ANNUAL UPDATE 2

UK POLITICS

Nick Gallop

HODDER EDUCATION
AN HACHETTE UK COMPANY

Orders: please contact Hachette UK Distribution, Hely Hutchinson Centre, Milton Road, Didcot, Oxfordshire, OX11 7HH. Telephone: +44 (0)1235 827827. Email education@hachette.co.uk. Lines are open from 9 a.m. to 5 p.m., Monday to Friday. You can also order through our website: www.hoddereducation.co.uk

ISBN: 978 1 3983 6122 5

First published in 2022 by
Hodder Education,
An Hachette UK Company
Carmelite House
50 Victoria Embankment
London EC4Y 0DZ

www.hoddereducation.co.uk

Impression number 10 9 8 7 6 5 4 3 2 1

Year 2026 2025 2024 2023 2022

Typeset in India

Printed by CPI Group (UK) Ltd, Croydon, CR0 4YY

A catalogue record for this title is available from the British Library.

Contents

Chapter 1

Pressure groups: lobbying in the 2020s – methods and controversies

Focus

Examination specifications focus on the methods that pressure groups, lobby groups and other collective organisations use to exert influence upon decision-makers in the UK. Students need to be able to analyse the characteristics of different types of groups, including think tanks, lobbyists and corporations, and evaluate their impact on government, politics and democracy in the UK.

Edexcel	UK Politics 1.3	Pressure groups and other influences
AQA	3.1.2.4	Methods used by pressure groups

Context

In 2021, the practice of lobbying by individuals and groups came under intense scrutiny after it was revealed that David Cameron, the former UK prime minister, who left Downing Street in 2016, had made contact with current ministers, including by repeated text messages to the chancellor Rishi Sunak, in his capacity as a paid adviser for Greensill Capital, a private financial services company.

Further to this, November 2021 saw the long-running investigation into the behaviour of Owen Paterson, Conservative MP for North Shropshire and former government minister, reach its dramatic conclusion. While Paterson was correct in declaring his paid positions providing consultancy to Randox Laboratories and Lynn's Country Foods, the Commissioner for Parliamentary Standards decided that his use of his parliamentary office and stationery for consultancy work, together with the sustained contact he had with officials at the Food Standards Agency and ministers at the Department for International Development, were 'serious breaches' of the rules governing lobbying activity in parliament. This is covered in more detail later in the chapter.

These controversies brought to the fore the highly contested influence of lobbying and lobbyists in the 2020s. Some argue that professional lobbyists are an essential part of a healthy democracy, ensuring that decision-makers are regularly informed about the latest developments, especially in fast-moving areas like science, technology and business. Others see them as a corruption of the system, providing wealthy, well-connected interests with a profoundly unfair advantage. Three key areas of analysis and evaluation are as follows.

- The Greensill Capital scandal in 2021 provides a contemporary insight into the world of lobbying, and is a valuable case study to support wider analysis of the changing methods employed by pressure groups. It also provides the opportunity to evaluate the extent to which lobbying activities by pressure groups and private companies support or undermine the political decision-making process.

- The Owen Paterson case remained in the headlines for several weeks in 2021 as it covered a number of controversial issues. The case led to: further revelations of the extent of paid 'consultancy work' undertaken by MPs; scrutiny of the role and work of the Commissioner for Parliamentary Standards and the House of Commons Standards Committee in monitoring alleged conflicts between MPs' professional roles and personal interests; concern about the fairness of the investigative process when MPs are found to be in breach of the rules; and criticism of the Conservative government's response in conflating Paterson's position with attempts to change the system for policing MPs' behaviour.
- On the opposite side, the transparency of government activity in engaging with lobby groups, and the effectiveness of parliamentary scrutiny in this area, is equally important to students of politics. The government review of lobbying activity related to Greensill Capital was published in July 2021, but for many commentators the main concerns lie in whether there is appetite for government and parliamentary reform.

Box 1.1 What is lobbying?

Lobbying is when individuals, groups, charities, businesses or trade unions try to influence the government to change its policies. Lobbying can take the form of personal meetings with ministers, MPs or officials plus letter-writing, emailing, or turning up in person to parliament to try to secure a meeting.

While any individual can attempt to influence decision-makers through lobbying, professional lobbying firms — often recruiting former politicians — usually have the contacts, the time and the resources to cultivate relationships with ministers, MPs and civil servants that are mutually beneficial.

Greensill Capital: when lobbying hit the headlines

The collapse of the private finance company Greensill Capital in March 2021 shone a spotlight on former prime minister David Cameron's close association with the company and his related lobbying activities.

Greensill Capital operated in the complicated world of 'supply chain finance'. Using enormous capital sums invested by trust funds, insurers and banks, Greensill Capital provided lucrative short-term loans to businesses, which are often caught without sufficient cash due to frequent delays of several months between selling goods and receiving payment for them.

When Greensill Capital collapsed in March 2021, the company filed for insolvency with billion-pound losses for investors and the loss of 440 jobs. However, it was revealed by the BBC that David Cameron had 'made about £3.3 million' from shares as a paid adviser to Greensill Capital and that he had been actively involved in persuading government ministers and senior civil servants to look favourably on the company.

Box 1.2 How did David Cameron lobby the government?

In 2020 David Cameron lobbied ministers, persuading them to permit Greensill Capital to join the Corporate Covid Financing Facility (CCFF), a scheme set up by the government to enable accredited finance companies to issue loans that were insured by the government and are therefore largely risk free to the loan companies advancing them. More specifically it was the manner of David Cameron's lobbying, and the unofficial access that he appeared to have to government ministers, that prompted widespread concern.

It was revealed that between March and June 2020, Cameron and his staff sent a total of 45 emails, texts and messages to ministers and senior civil servants. Of these, nine were Whatsapp messages to the chancellor Rishi Sunak, including requests for a 'quick word', pressure to include Greensill in the government-backed scheme, and requests for the chancellor to 'give it another nudge over the finish line'. Multiple messages to Tom Scholar, the Treasury's top civil servant, included texts such as:

> Hope you are still alive and well... Three questions: is Sir John C still at the bank? Do you have a number? Can I give you lunch once the budget is done? Love DC.

Other messages to Scholar included: '...please do all you can to expedite this and not let us get stuck in the pending tray!', 'I promise I will stop annoying you', and when the lobbying efforts were unsuccessful: 'Again Greensill have got a "no". Am genuinely baffled.'

The attempts to persuade ministers to allow Greensill Capital to join the government's Corporate Covid Financing Facility failed.

The collapse of the finance company and the revelations of David Cameron's active involvement in lobbying through unofficial channels caused widespread public anger in 2021. Indeed the 'Greensill Scandal' epitomised for many the seemingly exploitable network of personal contacts used by some former politicians, and the perception that the current Conservative government is more open to private business groups than it should be. In *The Times* (June, 2021) it was reported that 'dozens of lobbyists and business executives have far-reaching access to parliament under a free-for-all system' perpetuated by the Conservative government.

Box 1.3 What are the rules on former ministers lobbying the government?

The government sets out rules on how former ministers and senior crown servants should behave after leaving public office, with requirements that they seek advice from the Advisory Committee on Business Appointments (ACOBA) before accepting new jobs. In particular, ACOBA rules state that 'on leaving office, ministers will be prohibited from lobbying government for two years'. However, as is often stated, while former ministers are required to contact ACOBA, they are not required to follow its advice.

More stringent rules are regularly tabled, with ACOBA's current head, Lord Pickles, calling for former ministers who leave office to work as lobbyists to go on a register for 'up to 10 years' to ensure 'transparency'.

The Owen Paterson case: parliamentary standards and 'Tory sleaze'

The lobbying and private consultancy work of MPs remained stubbornly in the headlines throughout 2021, largely due to investigations into the activities of Owen Paterson. Paterson had been a Conservative MP since 1997, a member of the shadow cabinet since 2007, and in David Cameron's government as secretary of state for Northern Ireland between 2010 and 2012 and as secretary of state for environment, food and rural affairs between 2012 and 2014.

Since August 2015, Paterson had been a paid consultant to Randox, a clinical diagnostics company, and since December 2016 a paid consultant to Lynn's Country Foods, a processor and distributor of meat products. He earned £8,333 a month in return for 16 hours (per month) of consultancy work on behalf of Randox, and £12,000 per year in return for around 24 hours (per year) of consultancy work on behalf of Lynn's Country Foods.

Box 1.4 What did Owen Paterson do?

It was revealed by the BBC that Owen Paterson had made:

- three approaches to the Food Standards Agency for Randox about antibiotics in milk in 2016 and 2017
- seven approaches to the Food Standards Agency for Lynn's Country Foods in 2017 and 2018
- four approaches to ministers at the Department for International Development about Randox and blood testing technology in 2016 and 2017

In October 2019, the Parliamentary Commissioner for Standards opened an investigation into Paterson after allegations were made in the media that his lobbying activity was in breach of the rules. The profile of this investigation was substantially raised during the Covid-19 pandemic because:

- In March 2020, Randox secured a £133 million contract from the Department of Health and Social Care to produce testing kits.
- In September 2020, a £347 million government contract was awarded to Randox in a process that denied other companies the opportunity to bid.

In 2021, the investigation by the Parliamentary Commissioner for Standards into Owen Paterson's 'paid advocacy' (the use of privileged access for private gain) concluded that the MP had 'repeatedly used his privileged position to benefit two companies for whom he was a paid consultant, and that this has brought the house into disrepute'. This outcome, together with further declarations that 'no previous case of paid advocacy has seen so many breaches or such a clear pattern of behaviour in failing to separate private and public interests' was passed to the Commons Select Committee on Standards, which in turn recommended that Paterson be suspended from the House of Commons for 30 sitting days.

Box 1.5 What was Paterson's defence?

Owen Paterson sought to defend his behaviour by highlighting an exemption in lobbying rules for MPs whereby alerting government officials to 'serious wrong or substantial injustice' was acceptable, even if doing so would lead to financial benefit for the MP. While Paterson claimed that his advances fell into this category — especially in the context of the government's emergency response to the health pandemic — the Commissioner maintained that just one of his approaches to officials could be considered to have fallen within the exemption.

Box 1.6 How widespread is 'paid advocacy' in the House of Commons?

As long as MPs declare their private interests and earnings, they are permitted to perform other jobs and roles. Indeed, many MPs have other jobs as doctors, nurses, lawyers or advisers. However, the amount that many MPs earn in addition to representing their constituents in parliament and the time spent on these other roles is the subject of sustained controversy. In the aftermath of the Owen Paterson scandal, it was revealed that more than 200 MPs received earnings in the last year on top of their £81,932 annual salary. In the last year:

- Sir Geoffrey Cox (Conservative) earned around £900,000 in his work as a lawyer.
- Andrew Mitchell (Conservative) held six consultancy jobs with investment banks and accountancy firms, earning more than £180,000 for 35 days' work.
- Julian Smith (Conservative) earned £144,000 for 62–84 hours' work for three companies.
- Former transport and justice secretary Chris Grayling (Conservative) earned £100,000 to advise Hutchison Ports.

Source: adapted from news sites

In the aftermath of the recommendation by the Commons Select Committee on Standards, the Conservative Party was thrown into confusion. Many of Owen Paterson's Conservative Party allies saw the investigation process as unfair, with Paterson himself claiming that 'the process I have been subjected to does not comply with natural justice', highlighting the lack of any chance to appeal against the judgement.

Initially, prime minister Boris Johnson supported Owen Paterson by backing an amendment to the motion to suspend him. The amendment sought to pause the judgement in Paterson's case, to review the role of the Parliamentary Commissioner for Standards and the Commons' standards system, and to establish an appeals process. In a widely criticised move, Conservative whips instructed the party's MPs to support this amendment, which was passed by 250 votes to 232.

However, within a day and amid sustained accusations of 'Tory sleaze' as the government aimed to set aside the Standards Committee's judgement, Boris Johnson withdrew his support for the amendment and Owen Paterson immediately announced that he would be resigning as an MP. As it became apparent that opposition parties would not participate in the work of a new-styled select committee to investigate the disciplinary process for MPs, the leader of the House of Commons, Jacob Rees-Mogg, was left to admit that the best approach was to 'work with other parties' to make 'improvements' to the system.

Box 1.7 Parliamentary standards and Tory sleaze

The Conservative government's attempt to pause the judgement of the Standards Committee and overhaul its activity was widely considered to be both unethical and unprecedented. This, together with front-page revelations over the extent of paid consultancy work on the part of MPs, especially Conservative MPs, led to sustained accusations that the party had entered a new era of 'Tory sleaze'.

Additionally, many Conservative MPs were said to be 'furious' that they had been whipped to support an MP who most agreed had broken the rules. Mark Garnier, Conservative MP for Wyre Forest, said that he was 'incredibly unhappy about the government interfering in the business of the House in any way, shape or form'.

Should UK lobbying rules be reformed?

In 2014 the Office of the Registrar of Consultant Lobbyists (PRCA) was established and requires all people and organisations that lobby ministers or their permanent secretaries to register with it. While its aim is to ensure transparency in the work of lobbyists dealing with the government, those involved in 'incidental' contact, deemed to be 'minor accompaniments' to their wider roles with private companies, are exempt from registration.

Box 1.8 A former chancellor lobbies the Treasury

In August 2021 it was reported that the UK lobbying regulator was investigating whether former chancellor Lord Philip Hammond should have registered himself as a lobbyist when he contacted a top Treasury official with an offer from OakNorth Bank — a company that Lord Hammond advises — to promote bank-devised software that assessed the suitability of businesses seeking to take up Covid-related government loans and grants.

While Lord Hammond denied that his activity had effectively made him a 'lobbyist' and therefore subject to registration and rules, Francis Ingham, director-general of the Registrar of Consultant Lobbyists and an advocate for the strengthening of lobbying rules, described Hammond's reliance on the exemption as 'legalistic', adding that 'to a normal person it obviously doesn't bear scrutiny'.

However, accusations of a lack of transparency in the way that the government engages with business interests and in the securing of contracts continues. The Greensill Scandal led to the government commissioning an independent review into 'activities in government, and the role Greensill played in those', according to a Downing Street statement in April 2021.

The investigation by the Commons Treasury Committee resulted in several emphatic statements and recommendations, delivered in July 2021:

- Former prime minister David Cameron was accused of being 'too credulous' (gullible), demonstrating a 'lack of judgement' and being 'too willing to back the company without paying due diligence to its financial position'. The former prime minister's use of 'less formal means to lobby' demonstrated a 'significant lack of judgement'.
- The Treasury came in for criticism too. It 'should have encouraged Mr Cameron at the initial stage of his lobbying into more formal methods of communication' and, in light of the scandal, should 'put in place more formal processes to deal with any such lobbying attempts by ex-prime ministers or ministers in the future and to publish the process which they will follow should similar circumstances recur'.
- While the committee accepted that 'Mr Cameron did not break the rules governing lobbying by former Ministers', it asserted that this reflected the 'insufficient strength of the rules' and the 'strong case for strengthening them'.

However, chancellor Rishi Sunak also gave evidence to the committee and expressed his concern that firms 'may feel less able to engage with Ministers for fear of the public scrutiny'. Essentially, in certain sectors such as finance, cyber-security and intelligence gathering, private companies may feel inhibited from making contact with the government to propose specialist ideas or impart sensitive information. The committee acknowledged the need to balance this risk, but concluded that:

> ...those approaching Government for support from public finances for policies in their personal or corporate favour should expect public scrutiny and transparency. Any other approach runs the risk of appearing to be in conflict with good governance.

Comparisons and connections

- An interesting lobbying development in the USA in 2021 is the rise of the 'corporate coalition'. In September 2021 The *Washington Post* reported that 'corporate America' — including banking, technology, retail and pharmaceutical sectors, the US Chamber of Commerce, the National Association of Manufacturers and the Business Roundtable — had launched a 'lobbying blitz' to stop Congress from enacting significant parts of President Biden's $3.5 trillion dollar legislation which was set to reform the USA's health, education and social care systems.
- The strategy encompassed 'traditional lobbying' of legislators in Congress as well as concerted advertising campaigns designed to put pressure on Democratic lawmakers in the hope that the party's narrow congressional majority could be sufficiently unsettled. *The Post* referenced 'widely viewed ads on Facebook' that sought to highlight the damaging impact of future tax rises and threats to the country's post-Covid economic recovery, and that praised the 'nine moderate Democrats who had threatened to block the party's budget'.
- For further comparative examples, Open Secrets is one of the most extensive online resources for researching campaign contributions, lobbying data and analysis, its purpose being to 'track money in US politics and its effect on elections and public policy'.

Table 1.1 Is lobbying a beneficial part of the UK's pluralist democracy?

Yes	No
A basic lack of time, resources and skills prevents people from effectively representing their issues and concerns to policymakers. Organised lobbying — the gathering of like-minded individuals into a far more effective collective entity — provides people with a stronger voice and a better chance to improve their lives.	While some pressure group activity takes the form of mass popular movements, generating substantial media coverage, much of it is behind the scenes. Professional lobbyists (sometimes ex-MPs) are able to use privileged access to present one-sided or biased information to decision-makers.
In the USA, lobbying is seen as indivisible from healthy engagement in political life, protected by the First Amendment right 'to petition the government'. Similarly in the UK, the capacity to lobby the government encourages people to play an active role in the way they are governed. It is not lobbying that is the problem, but a lack of effective legislation to root out corruption and conflicts of interest.	The rules on lobbying in the UK need reforming. If the process of lobbying is to be seen as beneficial, many groups argue that a far longer ban on former cabinet ministers engaging in lobbying the government — from 2 to 5 years after leaving office — is required. In addition, all lobbyists working in any capacity should have to join the official lobbying register.
Studies of lobbying have demonstrated that it is more widespread and prevalent than generally accepted. The growing complexity of government, and the pace of social, political and technology change, have made lobbyists vital providers of information in the process of improving government policy and legislation.	Lobbying can only be seen as beneficial in the UK if the body that governs it is far stronger and supported by legislation. The Institute for Government (2021) recommends that the Advisory Committee on Business Appointments (ACOBA) is 'given a statutory footing' and the ability to 'fine people who do not seek the required approval, or who breach its conditions'.

What next?

Read: The Treasury Committee reports on 'Lessons from Greensill Capital', which can be found by searching on **https://committees.parliament.uk**

Read: The Commons Select Committee on Standards report on Owen Paterson, which can be found by searching for 'Committee on Standards' on **https://committees.parliament.uk**

Watch: 'David Cameron and the Missing Billions' on **www.bbc.co.uk**

Chapter 2

Rights in context: campaigns to protect liberties and to extend the franchise

Focus

Examination specifications require students to consider several areas related to rights. Students need to understand and evaluate the process by which the right to vote (the franchise) has been extended in the UK and, especially for those following the Edexcel specification, the work of a current movement to extend the franchise. In addition, students need to study the work and contributions of two contemporary civil liberty pressure groups.

Edexcel	1.2 and 1.4	The work of a current movement to extend the franchise; the work of two contemporary civil liberty pressure groups
AQA	3.1.1.1	Debates about the extent of rights in the UK

Context

While many traditional and well-established rights-based campaigns continue, such as those to support vulnerable and less visibly represented groups — the homeless, refugees and those with disabilities — many more issues connected to the influence and impact of technology have come to the fore. Online privacy rights, issues connected to mass surveillance, the use of facial-recognition software, the growth of requirements to possess identifying documentation such as photographic or biometric data — all feature in on-going campaigns to protect liberties and guard against what might be considered excessive state intrusion. Several on-going civil liberties movements developed further in the early 2020s including:

- Campaigns against government legislation to introduce mandatory voter identification: designed to make elections and voting more secure, yet argued to marginalise groups that do not have ready access to photographic ID.
- In the post-pandemic recovery, requirements to use vaccine passports and vaccine mandates were campaigned against as 'coercive' and 'punitive' by civil liberties groups.

In addition to the above campaigns relating to civil liberties, other movements seek to widen the franchise. In the recent past 16–17-year-olds have been enfranchised in certain regions of the UK and for certain elections, as have some categories of prisoners, and in 2021, calls intensified to give all EU residents — including those without settled status — who live, work and pay taxes in the UK, the right to vote in local elections in England and Wales.

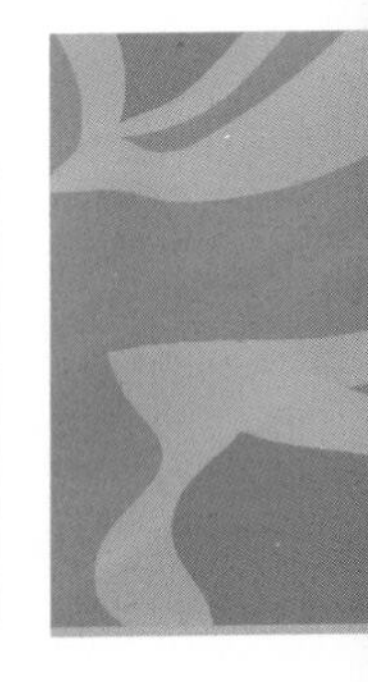

Box 2.1 Key definitions

Civil liberties: the rights with which a citizen of a state is endowed, usually guaranteed by a constitution or bill of rights.

The franchise: in democratic terms, the franchise is the right to vote; a 'contract' that exists between a citizen and the state which authorises them to vote in public elections.

Table 2.1 Examples of on-going civil liberties campaigns in the early 2020s

Campaign area	Explanation
Voter ID	Many groups and organisations such as the Electoral Reform Society campaigned against the government's Electoral Integrity Bill. Proposals to introduce mandatory voter ID were argued to threaten the basic right to vote. See Case study 1.
Vaccine passports and vaccine mandates	Civil liberties groups such as Liberty campaigned against proposals to introduce vaccine passports and vaccine mandates as 'coercive' and 'punitive'. See Case study 2.
Voting rights for EU citizens	While Scotland and Wales permit all EU residents, regardless of settled status, to vote in local elections, England and Wales do not. Groups such as the3million campaign for equal voting rights. See Case study 3.
Mass surveillance	The campaign against state surveillance powers developed when a coalition of human rights organisations won a landmark victory in May 2021 when the European Court of Human Rights declared government powers to intercept private communication 'unlawful'.
Policing and criminal justice	Groups such Friends of the Earth campaign against the government's Police, Crime, Sentencing and Courts Bill which is argued to threaten the rights of peaceful protest.
Emergency powers	Groups such as Big Brother Watch continue to campaign against the government's use of emergency powers and emergency measures in the wake of the health crisis.
ID verification and social media	A parliamentary petition to make verified ID a requirement for opening a social media account to prevent anonymised harmful activity and provide traceability if an offence occurs was signed by around 700,000 people in 2021.
Immigration and immigrants' rights	Many groups representing immigrants, refugees and other asylum rights organisations campaigned against the government's Nationality and Borders Bill which, the groups argued, would threaten basic human rights by removing traditional protections associated with refugee status.

Case study 1: The Electoral Reform Society and voter ID

The Electoral Reform Society (ERS) describes itself as a 'leading voice for democratic reform'. It campaigns to reform politics through two main goals:

1. To have public authorities in the UK elected by proportional representation and specifically by the single transferable vote in multi-member constituencies.
2. That the democratic institutions of the UK, its nations and regions and other constituent parts work in ways that lead to citizens having high levels of trust in them.

In June 2021 the government introduced legislation that would require voters to show voter ID in polling stations for UK parliamentary elections, local elections in England and police and crime commissioner elections in England and Wales. The requirements would not apply at Scottish Parliament and Senedd Cymru elections, nor local council elections in Scotland and Wales.

The types of ID required include passports, driving licences, PASS scheme and Blue Badge cards, and some travel passes. People without existing photo ID are able to apply for a free voter card from their local council to use in the polling station.

Opposition parties, particularly Labour, the Scottish National Party and many notable civil liberties groups, opposed the legislation on the grounds that the crime of pretending to be someone else when you vote is rare, and that the introduction of voter ID is an excessive measure likely to disproportionately affect already marginalised groups.

In 2021 the ERS criticised the government's legislation as 'an expensive distraction' and 'a sledgehammer to crack a nut'. It explained that unlike in many parts of mainland Europe where everyone has a mandatory national ID card, in the UK many citizens — those who cannot afford to go on foreign holidays (so have no specific need for a valid passport) or cannot drive (so have no access to photographic ID) — are disadvantaged. The ERS asserted that:

> Evidence from around the world shows that forcing voters to bring photographic ID to the polling station just makes it harder for people to vote – while doing little to increase faith in the integrity of the system. We don't need to spend millions to put up barriers to people taking part in our democracy.

The ERS campaigned to highlight several issues with the government's proposals, notably that:

- The government's own commissioned research found that those with severely limiting disabilities, the unemployed, people without qualifications and those who had never voted before were all less likely to hold any form of photo ID.
- The government's own figures suggest the scheme will cost up to an extra £20 million per general election.

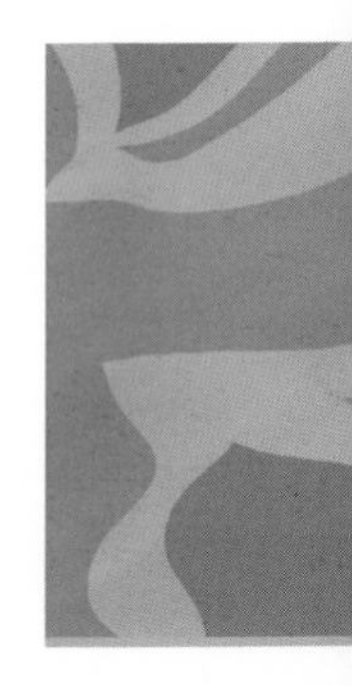

- Voting is already safe and secure in Britain:
  - First, public confidence in the running of elections is high. According to the Electoral Commission's latest tracker of public opinion, 80% of people are confident that elections are well run, 87% said voting in general is safe from fraud and abuse, and 90% said that voting at the polling station is safe.
  - Second, there are extremely low levels of electoral fraud in the UK. In 2019, there were just 33 allegations of impersonation at the polling station, out of over 58 million votes cast.

Case study 2: Liberty and vaccine passports

Liberty is an independent organisation that seeks to challenge injustice, defend freedom and provide policy responses on a wide range of issues that have implications for human rights and civil liberties.

As the vaccine roll-out took effect in the UK, Liberty campaigned against government proposals for 'vaccine passports' – potentially in the form of 'NHS Covid passes' — used as part of the UK's route out of pandemic-related restrictions.

In July 2021 Health Secretary Sajid Javid announced that businesses and large events would be 'encouraged', but not required, to use the vaccine passports. The government subsequently stated that it might consider mandating their use in some settings if 'sufficient measures are not taken to limit infection'.

In August 2021, Liberty rejected the notion that vaccine passports were an innocuous 'panacea', instead referring to them as a 'serious reinvention of our relationship to the state and potentially to our employers'. Liberty maintained that the understandable eagerness with which people embraced the vaccine programme should not be undermined by a 'coercive approach' that could marginalise those most confused by the often contradictory official messaging. In addition, those least trusting of government guidance, who also 'rely on work that is precarious', are the ones whose rights and autonomy would be most affected. Liberty explained that:

> If you face routine police discrimination, if you or members of your community have suffered from the hostile environment's web of surveillance that spreads through health care and other services, if you have been subjected to continuous failures in the welfare system, it might cause concern when asked to participate in Government programmes that affect your health choices, bodily autonomy and personal privacy.

In a move supported by the British Medical Association and the GMB Union, Liberty also highlighted the inception of 'vaccine mandates' for certain categories of workers, especially those involved in social care. Liberty explained that many who had 'risked their health and well-being on the frontline throughout this pandemic', those in precarious employment, yet often staffing critical sectors, were the most likely to face 'punitive measures'.

For Liberty, vaccine passports and vaccine mandates are the products of a government that prioritises 'coercion and punishment rather than care and support' and one that has 'failed to protect everyone equally'.

However, in September 2021:

- The Scottish first minister Nicola Sturgeon announced that in response to Scotland's 'fragile and serious' situation of record rises in Covid cases, vaccine passports would be required on entry to nightclubs, indoor live events with more than 4,000 unseated attendees, and any events hosting more than 10,000 people. Despite representatives of the nightclub sector criticising the scheme as 'not fit for purpose', enforcement of the vaccine passport scheme commenced on 18 October 2021.
- In England, Nadhim Zahawi, minister for Covid vaccine deployment, announced that 'vaccine passports' in nightclubs and other indoor venues in England would be required by the end of the month, as well as for sites with large crowds, as all over-18s would have been offered two jabs by then. However, a few days later on 12 September 2021, Sajid Javid, the health secretary, announced instead that plans to introduce vaccine passports for access into nightclubs and large events in England would not go ahead.

Case study 3: the3million and local voting rights for EU citizens

The Brexit referendum and the UK's subsequent departure from the European Union had a substantial impact on the UK's political landscape, not least for the millions of EU citizens living in the UK.

The campaign group the3million was formed after the referendum in 2016 and aimed to protect the rights of EU citizens who have 'made the UK their home'. Taking its name from the estimated number of EU citizens who have established a life in the UK, the3million seeks to:

- defend the rights of EU citizens to live, work, study, raise families and vote in the UK as they do now — whatever any further outcomes of Brexit
- protect EU citizens' rights through advocacy in UK and EU institutions, influencing public opinion and mobilising European and British citizens
- ensure that EU citizens in the UK know their rights and are empowered to stand up for them

The objectives of the3million range from providing legal support to citizenship advice, and in particular campaigning to extend rights for EU citizens to vote in UK elections.

Under the hashtag #OurHomeOurVote (**www.ourhomeourvote.co.uk**), the3million 'welcomes' the fact that EU citizens with pre-settled and settled status continue to have the right to vote in local elections in England and Northern Ireland, but campaigns for all EU citizens resident in the UK to be able to take part in local elections. The group's objectives are for England and Northern Ireland to adopt a residence-based voting rights system like those of Scotland and Wales, where all residents with leave to enter or remain in the UK are able to vote in local elections.

In August 2021, the *London Economic* covered a demonstration by the3million's Young Europeans Network and quoted its co-manager Lara

Parizotto who explained that 'it doesn't matter if you are a migrant, or someone born in the UK, you still have to pay local council tax. You use public transport, your local school, your local park, so it's only right that you get a say in how these services run'.

While many EU countries provide local voting rights to third country nationals, including British citizens, UK MPs have repeatedly rejected attempts to enfranchise many of the EU citizens residing in the UK. In August 2021, the UK government again withstood pressure to follow the example set by the devolved governments. The Elections Bill (2021) failed to support the campaign to provide all EU citizens resident throughout the UK, regardless of status, with equal voting rights in local elections.

Comparisons and connections

The protection of rights and the various campaigns to enhance civil rights are areas of the specifications that allow comparisons to be drawn between the USA and UK, with particular attention to the use of theoretical approaches to comparative politics — rational, structural and cultural.

- **Rational theories** stress differences in the enhancement and curtailment of rights in the USA and UK as being based mainly on political circumstances. For example, some of the most prominent civil rights legislation that influences modern-day politics in the USA was passed by President Lyndon B. Johnson in the 1960s, following the campaigns of the civil rights movement, in part led by Martin Luther King, and following the assassination of John F. Kennedy, whose political priorities had championed equal rights. There was no similar leadership or circumstances in the UK. On the other hand, the USA and UK responded similarly to heightened terror threats such as 9/11 by passing comparable legislation to enhance security measures and curtail former freedoms in the Anti-terrorism, Crime and Security Act 2001 (UK) and the Homeland Security Act 2002 (USA).
- **Structural theories** focus upon the institutional differences that exist between the UK and USA. The fact that the USA's constitution is both codified and entrenched serves to protect civil rights far more effectively than in the UK, where constitutional arrangements rely on a sovereign parliament to determine the full extent of rights. In addition, while the US Supreme Court is a constitutional court noted for its protection of rights, the UK Supreme Court is not.
- **Cultural theories** develop the roles that pressure groups play in enhancing and promoting civil rights. Key areas of similarity between the UK and USA include comparable levels of respect for the rule of law and the central importance of political pluralism. However, differences emerge in the significance of certain groups. While groups representing religions and races are generally understood to be more active and influential in the USA, those representing unionised workers are more prominent in the UK. Differences in rights-based political cultures also came to the fore during the health pandemic: in the USA anti-lockdown protests and resistance to government measures were far more widespread than in the UK, reflecting deeper levels of suspicion of government encroachment on civil liberties in America.

Exam success

Debates about the extent and protection of rights in the UK cut across several topics and the work of contemporary civil liberties groups is required to support wider analysis and evaluation.

The conflict between individual and collective rights remains a prominent feature of UK politics. Certain groups in society have very clear stances — potentially on religious, moral or cultural grounds — for living by the values and codes that they do. However, these stances can readily conflict with the rights of others to live and conduct themselves freely. While clashes have occurred around the globe as governments have imposed restrictive measures to control the health crisis, conflicts, for example between certain religious faiths and LGBTQ+ equality and between employees in fast-changing industries and their employment rights, have led to notable and protracted legal proceedings.

In addition, the UK's constitutional arrangements are geared to supporting freedoms and rights as demonstrated by respect for the independence of the judiciary and rule of law, and the fact that all legislation declares compatibility with the Human Rights Act (HRA). Contrary to this is the current lack of clarity characterised by debates over a 'British' Bill of Rights (to replace the Human Rights Act) and the tension that exists between legislation that promotes security and civil liberties campaigns discussed in this chapter.

What next?

Research: the campaigning work of the3million (**www.the3million.org.uk**), the Electoral Reform Society (**www.electoralreform.org.uk**) and Liberty (**www.libertyhumanrights.org.uk**)

Read: the history of changes to civil rights legislation in the UK at **www.politics.co.uk/reference/civil-liberties**

Read: 'The Elections Bill 2021: Summary factsheet', which can be found at **www.gov.uk**

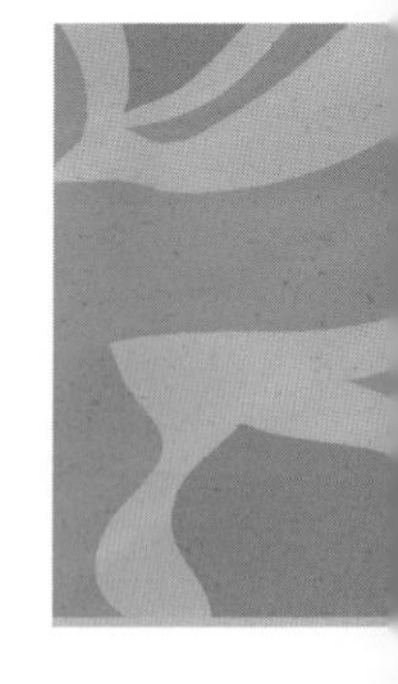

Chapter 3

Political parties: what does Keir Starmer's Labour Party stand for?

Focus

Examination specifications require thorough knowledge and understanding of the functions, features and funding of political parties. Alongside this, students need to be able to evaluate the importance of minor parties and the extent to which the UK has become a multi-party system. Perhaps most challenging of all is the need for students to understand the origins, ideas and historical development of the Conservative, Labour and Liberal Democrat parties and how these have shaped their ideas and current policies.

Pearson Edexcel	UK Politics 2.1–2.4	Political parties
AQA	3.1.2.3	Political parties

Context

In September 2021, Keir Starmer addressed the Labour Party Conference in person for the first time since his leadership had begun early in 2020. This timespan clearly reflects the fact that the Labour leader's early tenure had been entirely overshadowed by the Covid-19 pandemic, making his ability to define a distinctive leadership 'style', or 'cut through' on policies considered to be more relevant than those related to health, extremely difficult.

That aside, commentators often draw attention to perceived inconsistencies in the Labour leader's approach. On the one hand, the summer of 2020 saw a 'dizzyingly large' number of Labour Party policy statements, with sometimes two major announcements in one day. While the policy blitz was designed to add substance to Starmer's leadership, it left many people without a clear idea of what Labour under Starmer stood for.

On the other hand, a year late in September 2021, the Conservative Party unveiled controversial policies to reform social care, but no alternative was proposed by the Labour Party. In an area that represents one of the most important areas of party strategy, the *New Statesman* posed the question: 'Why hasn't Keir Starmer told us where Labour stands on social care?'

For students of politics, establishing discernible directions and themes within the Labour Party under Keir Starmer is important in order to determine what the party currently stands for, and the extent to which Labour's 'core values' are evident in party policy.

Box 3.1 Labour's 'core values'

While policies and priorities have adapted over time, the origin of the Labour Party, as the parliamentary wing of the trade union movement, is still relevant to its principles and values to this day. Redistributive taxes to lessen wealth inequality; a commitment to public ownership of important industries; a generous welfare state supporting health, education and other benefits; and strong protection of employment and union rights are all representative of the party's core values.

What has happened to the Labour Party?

Sir Keir Starmer became Labour Party leader at the start of one of the most complex and challenging periods in modern UK history. In April 2020, and less than 2 weeks into the UK's first period of national lockdown due to the spread of the coronavirus, Starmer won the party leadership contest. Subsequently, he began his mission to recover from the party's disastrous 2019 general election defeat just 4 months earlier, and rebuild the party into a credible alternative to prime minister Boris Johnson's then buoyant Conservatives.

Box 3.2 Keir Starmer

Named after the legendary first leader of the Labour Party, Keir Hardie, Starmer is the son of a nurse and toolmaker who became an eminent lawyer and QC, latterly as Director of Public Prosecutions and the Head of the Crown Prosecution Service. He became an MP in 2015 and Labour leader in 2020.

At the outset, the primary area of contention was the extent to which Keir Starmer was going to embrace or reject Jeremy Corbyn's legacy. Corbyn, the former Labour leader, had re-energised support within the party for a much more socialist programme. The late wave of support for a Corbyn-led Labour Party in the run-up to the 2017 general election, one that saw the Conservatives' hard-won majority of 2015 wiped out and a Labour gain of 30 seats, had convinced many that it was a programme that could achieve electoral success.

However, to understand the uncertain circumstances that the Labour Party found itself in early in the 2020s, an understanding of the changing direction of the party since the 1980s is needed — see Box 3.3.

Box 3.3 Labour since the 1980s

Prior to the 2019 general election, the 1980s stood as the most remarkable low point for the Labour Party. Architects of the modern welfare state in the 1940s, and in-and-out of government following that, the Labour Party had spent a disastrous 18 years in opposition between 1979 and 1997.

The party's socialist agenda of the early 1980s — with calls to vastly increase tax rates, renationalise industries, withdraw from the European Union and abolish the UK's nuclear defence — was heavily at odds with an increasingly optimistic and affluent electorate. A fourth general election defeat in 1992 heralded a radical rethink to broaden the party's appeal.

From the mid-1990s, New Labour's 'Third Way' under Tony Blair advocated an acceptance of aspects of a free-market economy as a necessary part of Britain's global future. This, together with moves to limit the scope of the welfare state but with sustained investment in health and education, and a much more restrained approach to personal and corporate taxation, appealed to many more voters, resulted in three successive general election victories (including the landslides of 1997 and 2001, delivering overwhelming governing majorities), but served to alienate more 'traditional' Labour supporters.

Fast forward to the latter years of the 2010s and disillusionment with the inequalities of capitalism and a free-market economy saw Jeremy Corbyn's socialist programme have greater appeal, especially to younger votes. But Corbyn's personal unpopularity and the apparent radicalism of his past, concerns about excessive public spending under a Corbyn government, a lack of clarity over Brexit, and a failure to connect with more socially conservative voters in the former Labour heartlands of the Midlands and the North resulted in catastrophic defeat in 2019. In securing just 202 seats (to the Conservatives' 365) it was the Labour Party's worst postwar general election performance.

While the story of all political parties the world over is one of continual reinvention and renewal in response to ever-changing social, political and economic challenges — usually accompanied by accusations of 'selling out' through change, or 'obsolescence' through clinging to traditional values — the British Labour Party has struggled more than most to remain aligned to its socialist roots yet to define itself clearly and attractively in a fast-changing, globalised world.

Labour under Starmer: objectives and achievements

Early in his leadership, Keir Starmer was keen to push away comparisons with predecessors, especially questions over whether his ideas and ambitions were more aligned to Jeremy Corbyn's socialist agenda or to Tony Blair's much more 'centrist' interpretation of the party's values. Descriptive words about Starmer such as 'thoughtful' and 'serious' tended to proliferate — as did a sense that while there was a genuine desire to tackle inequality and poverty and to improve people's lives, the means to do so remained steadfastly unclear.

In a 2020 BBC interview, political editor Laura Kuenssberg highlighted the difficult job that Starmer faced. He needed to 'distance himself' from the failure of Labour under Corbyn, as symbolised by the 2019 election manifesto, while not alienating many of the Labour voters who believed strongly in that agenda and who would still form the bedrock of the party's support in a 2024 general election.

The main directions of Keir Starmer's first years as leader revolve around putting an end to the damaging factional rivalry within the Labour Party, rooting out the destructive forces of anti-Semitism that had plagued the party under Jeremy Corbyn's leadership and establishing his own distinctive agenda.

Ending division and uniting the party

Division and factional rivalry are characteristics of all long-standing political parties, the modern Labour Party more so than most. Controlling the rise and fall of key organisations that exist under Labour's broad umbrella has posed a challenge for all Labour leaders, with battle lines currently drawn between 'hard left', socialist, Corbyn-supporting groups, and those that champion the centre-left aspirations of more moderate members. Ending the rivalry and uniting most groups within the party around an agenda that is internally supported and externally electable is the single most important challenge for Keir Starmer.

Table 3.1 Left, soft-left and centre-left — larger factions within the Labour Party in the 2020s

Left or soft-left factions	Centre-left or 'moderate' factions
Momentum: while significantly diminished after the election of Starmer, the group that had its origins in the socialist resurgence led by Jeremy Corbyn still has a large membership and full-time staff. Formed in 2015, it is estimated to have around 40,000 members.	**Labour First:** an influential group under Starmer's leadership. Founded in the 1980s it is an older centre-left group with strong links to trade unions and local government. Under Corbyn's leadership, Labour First settled differences with New Labour supporters and united in opposition to the former leader's policy priorities.
Forward Momentum: the controlling faction within Momentum has changed the group's direction from 'winning elections' to empowering grassroots supporters with initiatives like 'policy primaries' that allow members to vote on the priorities they want the party to adopt.	**Labour to Win (L2W):** a union of **Labour First** and **Progress**, which was established in 1996 to champion New Labour. The aim of the group was to link all centre-left groups with the common aim of 'moving on' from Corbynism and energising the electability of Labour under Keir Starmer.
Open Labour: a 'soft-left' faction founded in 2015 but that has struggled to gain a foothold. Its promotion of more open debate and less in-fighting within the party, and its toleration of a more pluralist approach have hampered its own development in a bitterly divided party.	**Progressive Britain:** after the launch of L2W, Progress merged with Peter Mandelson's Policy Network and become Progressive Britain. Progressive Britain has focused more on research and generating policy positions, to energise the centre-left and moderate party membership.

In August 2021, *The Guardian* reported that 'despite the leader's promise to end factionalism', rivalry and internal division were 'alive and well' within the Labour Party. However, it did reveal what could be the start of a several-year process of ousting the organisations and factions within Labour that are critical of Keir Starmer. Four groups ejected from the Labour Party in the summer of 2021 were:

- **Socialist Appeal**: a Trotskyist group considered a successor to Militant (a hard-line Marxist wing within the Labour Party that advocated a radical anti-capitalist, socialist agenda)
- **Labour Against the Witch-hunt:** a group that believes anti-Semitism claims within Labour were made up to smear Jeremy Corbyn and his supporters

- **Labour in Exile Network:** a group set up to harbour and defend individuals suspended or expelled from Labour
- **Resist:** a group set up by ex-MP Chris Williamson attempting to register as a rival political party

While the group expulsions only affected around 1,000 individual party members, Starmer's intention to steadily move the party 'back' to the centre, working closely with Labour to Win, and promoting into the shadow cabinet MPs with centre-left credentials at the expense of 'left-wing' former Corbyn-allies such as Rebecca Long Bailey, appears to be increasingly evident.

'Rooting out' anti-Semitism

On accepting the leadership, Keir Starmer condemned what he referred to as the 'stain' of anti-Semitism within the Labour Party and avowed his intention to 'tear out this poison by its roots'. In holding meetings with Jewish groups (including the Board of Deputies, the Jewish Leadership Council, the Community Security Trust and the Jewish Labour Movement) within days of his election, Starmer was praised in a joint statement by those groups as having achieved 'in four days more than his predecessor in four years in addressing anti-Semitism within the Labour Party'.

Since then, Keir Starmer has responded assertively to a report by the Equality and Human Rights Commission (EHRC) into allegations of anti-Semitism and harassment within Labour Party. It gave a damning verdict and highlighted breaches of the Equality Act amid 'a culture within the party which, at best, did not do enough to prevent anti-Semitism and, at worst, could be seen to accept it'.

In response, Keir Starmer released a detailed plan for tackling anti-Semitism in the Labour Party, committing again to the already-established independent complaints process and to addressing the 'backlog' of anti-Semitism cases. In addition, high-profile suspensions of members, including Jeremy Corbyn, and a robust challenge to allegations that anti-Semitism in the party is 'exaggerated' have led many Jewish groups to continue to praise Starmer's approach.

Delivering a distinctive agenda

In early 2020, Keir Starmer's leadership campaign focused upon 'Ten Pledges' based on what he referred to as 'the moral case for socialism'. The pledges included increasing tax on the top 5% of earners, abolishing Universal Credit (the unpopular welfare payment system established by the Conservative Party), and commitments to public service ownership, devolved power, tackling climate change, human rights and the rights of migrants.

Since then, and most notably in September 2021 ahead of the Labour Party Conference, Keir Starmer published an 11,500-word essay on what he stands for and how he wants to lead a UK that is 'crying out for change'. In a bid to silence critics accusing him of lacking vision and direction, Starmer's wide-ranging pamphlet had several targets, including:

- An emphasis on 'putting families first' by highlighting better levels of 'security and opportunity' through sustained investment in skills and stable jobs.

- Branding prime minister Boris Johnson as 'utterly unserious and completely unprepared for the great challenges of our time'.
- Accusing the Conservative Party and the SNP of being 'in thrall to nationalism' and stating that Labour's stance could be 'proudly patriotic' while 'rejecting the divisiveness of nationalism'.

Within the collection of policy priorities in the first 2 years of Starmer's leadership, there were some more traditionally socialist strands. These were most evident in the commitment to higher taxes on the wealthy and on businesses, a recommitment to nationalisation, and significant public investment in education and healthcare. However, alongside these sit some notable links to New Labour's agenda such as constitutional reform, enhanced rights and devolution. The renewed focus on patriotism and the dropping of a previous Starmer pledge to reintroduce free movement within the EU as 'impossible' can be seen as policies designed to appeal to former Labour voters, particularly those concerned about their communities changing though unchecked immigration, and about wages being kept low by the availability of temporary workers from overseas.

The early 2020s was a difficult time for any Opposition leader to gain traction. The health crisis and the low point for Labour of the 2019 general election certainly provided the most unstable of bases from which to launch a radical plan of action. While Keir Starmer did deliver an effective 2021 Conference speech, and is praised for tackling anti-Semitism within the party, most commentators point to the long road ahead — and especially to the need for significantly better approval ratings if he is to be in a position to win a general election campaign in 2024.

Exam success

Examination questions on this topic can range widely, but many may focus on the extent to which the Labour Party has departed from its socialist roots in recent years. It is an angle that requires students to have at least an 'overview' level of understanding of the development of the party since the 1980s and to be able to contrast the direction that Jeremy Corbyn's leadership took the party in after New Labour and Keir Starmer's direction since then. Questions may be framed as follows:

- *Evaluate the view that the Labour Party is no longer a socialist party.* (30 marks, Edexcel style).
- *'The current Labour Party has departed significantly from its original socialist principles in an attempt to win voters.' Analyse and evaluate this statement.* (25 marks, AQA style).

Evaluation and analysis will include aspects of the following:

- Within this chapter is a brief overview of the policies and priorities of **New Labour under Blair and Brown** that took the party in significantly different directions from the Labour Party of the 1980s and before. Changes in class and employment structures, alongside heavy election defeats in the 1980s, resulted in a substantial modernisation process under Tony Blair — a modernisation in substance (such as an end to nationalisation commitments, a decline in the role of the trade union movement, an acceptance of the free market and private–public partnerships) and in style (a 'rebranding' to make the party more friendly to potential middle-class voters with a progressive agenda for the protection of rights and constitutional reforms). For many Labour-supporting opponents of New Labour, Blair's project was branded 'Thatcherism with a human face' — a contradictory phenomenon that nevertheless proved electorally popular until Gordon Brown's defeat in 2010.

- The most effective evaluation of Labour in the following decade comes in the form of the 2019 Labour Party general election manifesto which contained far more authentically socialist commitments than those under Blair. The **Jeremy Corbyn-led Labour Party** pledged to increase the NHS budget by 4.3%, cut back on private provision in the public sector, renationalise many major industries such as energy, transport and the Royal Mail (economic socialism), commit to net-zero carbon emissions by the 2030s, enhance protection for refugees and asylum seekers (globalist internationalism), and strengthen the powers of trade unions and workers' rights (traditional trade unionism).
- It is harder to establish the direction of **Labour under Keir Starmer**. Starmer has only been an MP since 2015 and Labour leader since early 2020. There are some policy directions in the 'objectives and achievements' section of this chapter and there are also some clues in Starmer's pre-MP professional life to indicate his strength of support for the Human Rights Act, and his commitment to social justice, equality and defending the rights of marginalised groups, especially evidenced in his role as Director of Public Prosecutions.

What next?

Read: the article 'New Labour 20 years on: assessing the legacy of the Tony Blair years', an effective evaluation of the legacy of New Labour, *The Conversation,* **https://theconversation.com**

Read: 'It's time for a real change: the Labour Party manifesto 2019', **https://labour.org.uk**

Read: 'The road ahead', Keir Starmer's essay, which appears to set Labour on course for the 'centre ground', **https://fabians.org.uk**

Chapter 4

Political parties (Part 2): are the Tories under Boris Johnson really 'one-nation conservatives'?

Focus

Examination specifications require students to understand the origins, ideas and historical development of the major parties. For the Conservative Party, this requires knowledge and evaluation of one-nation conservatism, and of how modern interpretations of the party's traditional values have led to periods of both consensus and division.

Edexcel	2.1–2.4	Political parties
AQA	3.1.2.3	Political parties

Context

In 2021, many commentators saw confirmation of a new era for Conservative Party policy. For several years, and certainly since the 2019 general election victory, Boris Johnson has sought to distance the Conservative Party from the austerity years of the 2010s, branded by the former governor of the Bank of England Mark Carney as 'the first lost decade since the 1860s'. In place of austerity and hardship was to be 'an economy fit for a new age of optimism', as announced by chancellor Rishi Sunak when delivering his autumn 2021 budget in the House of Commons.

Boris Johnson has regularly proclaimed the government's commitment to 'levelling up' and 'building back better' with a pledge to increase public spending levels to those not seen since the 1950s. In order to afford the investment needed to realise this, however, the Office for Budget Responsibility estimates that the tax burden (the amount of tax paid by a person, business or nation as a proportion of total income) is set to rise from its pre-pandemic level of around 33% of GDP to over 36% by 2026. The main consequence of this is a significantly growing tax burden for households and businesses.

Commitments to spend the largest proportion of GDP on public spending since the 1970s, along with levels of personal and corporation taxes not seen since the 1950s, have led many to conclude that the Conservative government is entering a new and distinct phase of 'one-nation conservatism'. But questions remain over quite what this concept means, whether the current brand of conservatism fits the one-nation model, and what the unique challenges and implications are for a Conservative government committed to 'one-nation conservatism' in the 2020s.

Box 4.1 Key definition

Austerity: after the financial crisis of 2007/08, economic measures were introduced in the UK that echoed a similar period of 'austerity' immediately following the Second World War. The 2010s became known as 'the age of austerity', associated with the Conservative Party in power from 2010 onwards. Cuts to welfare payments, housing subsidies and social services aimed to reduce the government's budget deficit but caused hardship for many.

One-nation conservatism: with its origins in policies driven by prime minister Benjamin Disraeli from the late 1800s, one-nation conservatism refers to an approach adopted by the British Conservative Party accentuating the responsibilities of a ruling elite to improve the lives of all members of society, regardless of class or status. One-nation conservatism emphasises the paternalistic role and responsibilities of leaders to engage fully with the interests of all, rather than solely with those interests of the upper and business classes.

What is one-nation conservatism?

Similar to the evolutionary nature of conservatism itself, the one-nation concept of conservatism has evolved and developed for almost two centuries. At its core lies the duty of privileged leaders to ensure that those less fortunate are supported through concerted social and economic programmes to improve their lives. Two recognisable periods of one-nation conservatism are often cited:

- In the late 1860s, prime minister and Conservative leader Benjamin Disraeli pushed a raft of social reforms through parliament in a bid to improve the lives of working-class people and to better protect workers. The 1867 Reform Act began to enfranchise working-class men, so Disraeli's one-nation conservatism was opportunistic as well as ethical. In the same way that Edmund Burke argued that society is not static and often must 'change to conserve' itself, in his famous Crystal Palace speech of 1872 Disraeli spoke of a new direction and of 'the elevation of the condition of people'. In an era of rapid industrialisation, laws to protect workers and clean up cities characterised this period of one-nation conservatism.
- In the postwar period of the 1950s and early 1960s, Conservative prime ministers Winston Churchill, Anthony Eden and Harold Macmillan all sought to redefine conservatism as committed to narrowing social inequality, supporting and developing the modern welfare state created under Labour's Clement Attlee. In particular, Macmillan's leadership (1957–63) saw a reframing of both one-nation conservatism and paternalism in ways that resonate to the present day. Like Disraeli and Burke before him, Macmillan highlighted the debilitating effects of unemployment, and the threat it posed to social and economic stability.

Box 4.2 Paternalism

Paternalism is a practice of the state managing or governing society in an outwardly benevolent way for individuals. Conservatism has an ambivalent attitude to paternalism. While acknowledging that the state should intervene to assist individuals there remains a debate, particularly with one-nation and neo-conservatives about the extent of state intervention. To differing degrees, all aspects of conservatism are concerned that paternalism treats adults as if they were children, which can both arrest their development and leave individuals reliant on the state.

Source: adapted from David Tuck, 'Paternalism and conservatism', *Politics Review*, Vol. 31, No. 2, November 2021

The aftermath of both these periods saw a lengthy reassertion of more free-market capitalist traditions within the Conservative Party and an avoidance of paternalist approaches. Such fluctuations highlight the fact that, while one-nation and paternalist approaches have been highly influential within the development of conservatism, they have been far from dominant.

Box 4.3 Neo-conservatism

Neo-conservatism is a variation of conservatism that emphasises some aspects of traditional conservative values such as law and social order, along with a reduction in the responsibilities of the state in terms of welfare support and public investment, and an emphasis on an assertive foreign policy to defend and promote democratic values abroad.

Indeed, for neo-conservative leaders like Margaret Thatcher, the 'dependency culture' created by generous welfare state-sponsored paternalism was argued to have arrested individual development, creating and sustaining an underclass of people dependent on the state and content to live off welfare benefits. Such influences within the Conservative Party were evident as recently as in the UK Welfare Reform Act of 2012, designed to incentivise those dependent on welfare to go back to work by bringing in more means-tested benefits.

What does one-nation conservatism mean in the 2020s?

In the 2020s, there are a number of echoes of the last recognisable period of one-nation conservatism and also some significant challenges for a Conservative government that seeks to emphasise its 'one-nation' credentials. Four key areas of where the government might be seen to be taking a one-nation approach to current challenges are:

- the government's acknowledgment of its responsibility actively to tackle inequality, especially regional inequality
- the rising level of investment in public services in order to support disadvantaged social groups
- redefining 'Britishness' and the UK's foreign policy priorities in the wake of Brexit, the health pandemic and global uncertainty
- an appreciation that both the Conservative Party and its policies must represent and support the interests of all, regardless of race, class, gender, sexuality or disability

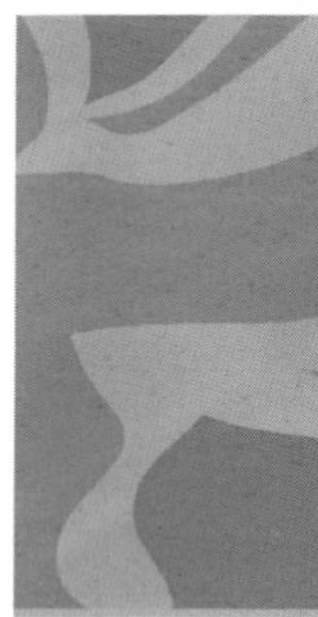

Tackling regional inequality

One of the most striking outcomes of the 2019 general election was the redrawing of the electoral map of the UK. Many communities and constituencies that had formerly supported the Labour Party, some for many generations, returned a Conservative MP. Dozens of so-called 'red wall' seats in the Midlands and north 'turned blue'. Wrexham, Workington, Blyth Valley; swathes of the West Midlands, Yorkshire, Lancashire and the northeast — seats that had evaded even Margaret Thatcher's 1980s landslides — were won by the Conservatives in 2019.

Needless to say, with new support from new areas of the UK came new expectations and considerable responsibilities for a Conservative Party long seen as willing to ignore Labour-voting regions in favour of its southern, traditionally Conservative heartlands. While one-nation conservativism places the narrowing of class-based inequality between rich and poor at its heart, the Conservative Party of the 2020s regularly professes a commitment to tackling *regional* inequality.

Box 4.4 Tackling regional inequality

One of the worst countries in the world for regional inequality, Britain has seen a disproportionate yet necessarily high level of investment in infrastructure and employment in London and the South East, but often overlooked working class and coastal communities in the north of England, Wales and Scotland. In 2017, average disposable income in London stood at £28,000 p.a., compared to just £16,000 in the North East. To be a one-nation conservative in the 2020s should mean a commitment to investing in infrastructure projects in underfunded regions of the UK, improving standards of education in these areas and empowering local communities.

Source: Ollie Tinker, 'What should "one-nation conservatism" mean in the 2020s?' Bright Blue, April 2020. Bright Blue is a Conservative think tank.

Boris Johnson's 'levelling up' mantra to reduce regional inequality has seen him commit the government to major infrastructure projects. These include transport schemes linking north to south, attracting employers to areas of high unemployment, and the creation of freeports to boost trade in less developed areas. In November 2021, the transport secretary Grant Shapps reaffirmed the government's commitment to spend £96 billion on transforming transport services in the Midlands and northern England.

Box 4.5 UK government policy on freeports

The Conservative Party Manifesto included a commitment to create up to ten freeports around the UK. According to the Government, freeports are intended to be national hubs for global trade and investment across the UK. They also aim to promote regeneration and job creation as part of the Government's policy to level up communities. Finally, the Government sees them as hotbeds for innovation.

Source: House of Commons briefing paper on freeports, May 2021

While there is little doubt of the intent, the *Financial Times* in November 2021 reported that the prime minister was 'facing uproar' from civic leaders and Tory MPs in northern England as he appeared to 'water down' commitments to the High Speed 2 (HS2) railway and plans for an entirely new Leeds–Manchester line. For many, effective connections between formerly underinvested regions, on a par with transport networks in London and the southeast, are central to tackling regional inequality. Yet scrapping essential elements such as the East Midlands–Leeds leg of HS2 has left many people in key regions feeling 'betrayed'.

Investing in public services

Many commentators point to a distinct change in Conservative policy under Boris Johnson. It is a shift that has repositioned the party away from the 'fiscal conservatism' of the Thatcher era — low taxes and 'responsible' levels of low public spending — and towards a 'fiscal expansionist' model of higher taxes and higher spending. This is a move that is said to have reclaimed the 'centre ground' and a public spending profile that many have likened to the one-nation conservatism of the 1950s and, more recently, the centrist 'New Labour' policies of the late 1990s and early 2000s. While public spending shrank dramatically during the 1980s — from 41% of GDP in 1980 to under 35% of GDP in 1990 — the Office for Budget Responsibility (OBR) projects public spending to be back at nearly 42% by 2026. In addition, the OBR notes that this represents 'the largest sustained share of GDP since the late 1970s' — an era that was, of course, followed by a fierce reduction in state spending in the 1980s under Margaret Thatcher.

Box 4.6 Fiscal conservatism or one-nation conservatism?

In June 2021, Andrew Neil on GB News tackled chancellor Rishi Sunak on the question of whether he was a 'one-nation', 'big government' Conservative 'like the prime minister' or a 'small government, fiscal Conservative'. Sunak reaffirmed his credentials as a 'fiscal Conservative' but one intent on delivering 'our commitments in the manifesto to invest in public services' and 'to spread opportunity around the country'.

Just as previous periods of one-nation conservatism had, this same apparently conflicted approach in conservatism continues to generate considerable tension within the wider Conservative Party — between those 'worried about a new era of high-spending Tory government', and those 'who fancy a bit of that big spending for their constituencies or pet policy issues'.

Source: adapted from Isabel Hardman, 'Rishi Sunak: I'm a fiscal Conservative (unlike Boris)', *The Spectator*, June 2021

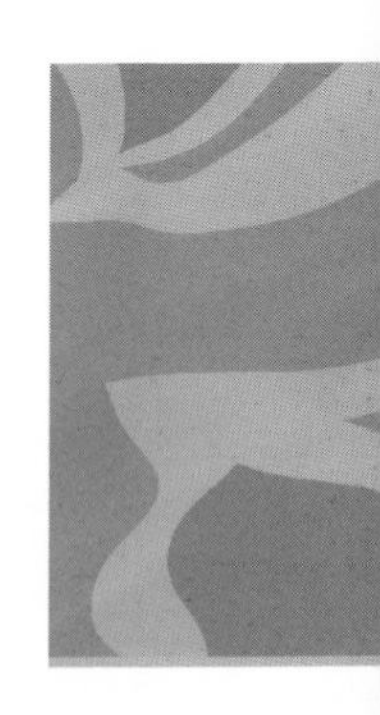

The union, Britishness and foreign policy

Part of the one-nation tradition is a strong sense of collective identity and endeavour, with patriotism and a sense of 'Britishness' playing a significant part. Indeed, for many who talk about the benefits of a one-nation conservative approach, the two concepts — of 'one-nation conservatism' and of 'what it means to be British' — are intertwined.

The future of the union is arguably the most contested area of domestic politics. When Boris Johnson proclaimed himself 'minister for the union', it was recognised that he was burnishing his one-nation credentials by pledging to protect the union and emphasising its mutual benefits for all nations and regions.

However, in the immediate aftermath of a 2019 general election result that Boris Johnson proclaimed as a victory for 'one-nation conservatism', Ian Macwhirter in the Scottish *Herald* cautiously agreed, emphasising that Boris Johnson had inadvertently spoken the truth. The victory did 'apply in only one nation: England'. Macwhirter further emphasised that 'Scotland is now, in a very real sense, another country'. The direction of travel in a post-devolved UK, one in which resurgent Scottish nationalism is a permanent feature, as is a feeling of disconnection between London and much of the rest of the UK, has led some to conclude that the very best one-nation conservatives can hope for is a fully federal UK.

In addition, just as in the 1950s when Conservative leaders sought to re-establish the UK's place in the world after the trauma and turbulence of world war and imperial disintegration, the protracted ordeal of the UK's departure from the European Union presents both opportunities and challenges for the Conservative Party in foreign affairs. Some argued that the historic security pact signed by the UK, USA and Australia (AUKUS) in September 2021 to counter the military reach of China in the Indo-Pacific region is an example of the re-establishment of the UK, working with traditional allies on the global stage.

One-nation conservatism and inclusivity

A criticism that has perennially afflicted the Conservative Party is that its policies speak first and foremost to a solidly wealthy, middle-class section of the electorate. One of the biggest issues of the 2020s, for any party rebranding itself as truly 'one nation', is to rise to the multiple challenges of the economic and social impact of the health crisis and the influence and effect of recent social movements based around race and gender.

Britain is a vast, multi-faith, multi-racial community in which around 14% of the population is from minority ethnic backgrounds, with significant concentrations in many local and regional populations. It is a UK wholly unlike that of the 1950s, the last recognisable period of one-nation conservatism. In modern Britain, truly one-nation policies designed to narrow inequalities are not class-based, but ones that promote inclusivity, equality and tolerance and that recognise the true level of diversity — in all senses — of the British population.

That said, the Conservative Party has elevated both of the two women to have become British prime ministers and currently, at least in terms of ethnicity, it has one of the most diverse cabinet memberships with a chancellor, home secretary and attorney general of Asian descent, and a black business secretary and foreign office minister. However, further representative change is required. In the Conservative Party's Commons ranks, just 22 of the 65 MPs are from minority ethnic backgrounds, while other vital representative markers — such as gender, sexuality and disability — are well known to require addressing.

Box 4.7 Black, British and Conservative

The members opposite claim Windrush as their own. As if it is obvious that immigrants are somehow obliged, morally and practically, to be Labour supporters. Well, my family was not — and I am not. I stand here as evidence of what immigrants, and their children, can achieve in what my parents called the land of opportunity. I am proud to be the first Conservative MP of West Indian heritage. Black, British with all my heart, immensely proud of my West Indian heritage and Conservative to my fingertips.

Darren Henry, Conservative MP for Broxtowe, House of Commons maiden speech, June 2020

Comparisons and connections

There are significant areas of likely comparison when it comes to recognising similar and distinct trends within the 'conservative' parties of the UK and USA. In particular:

- In both the UK and USA, tensions within the conservative 'right' remain over one-nation and neo-conservatism approaches. The sustainability of a generous welfare system is a key concern of neo-conservatives in both the UK and USA, largely down to the levels of individual and corporate taxation that are required to make it sustainable. Consequently, Republicans in the USA continue to oppose a publicly funded healthcare system and in the UK neo-conservative ideas such as means-tested benefits, higher tuition fees and less generous state pensions are all features of Conservative Party policy.
- Yet the last three UK prime ministers, David Cameron, Theresa May and Boris Johnson, have all described themselves as one-nation conservatives, distancing themselves from a Republican Party that is far more neo-conservative in outlook. For instance, in both the UK and USA, while one-nation conservatives and neo-conservatives embrace the paternalistic welfare state, commitment to considerably increased investment, by all measures, is far more evident in the UK.
- The health crisis saw extensive use of the 'one-nation', paternalistic policy of furloughing in the UK to protect employees and the self-employed from the financial fallout of the crisis, with over £100 billion spent on the scheme. While the more neo-conservatist, small-state outlook of the Republican Party was more restrained in its direct support to employees, Republicans did back the Coronavirus Aid, Relief and Economic Security Act (2020) (CARES Act) under the presidency of Donald Trump, indicating a similar ideological commitment to the preservation of the organic state in both the USA and UK.

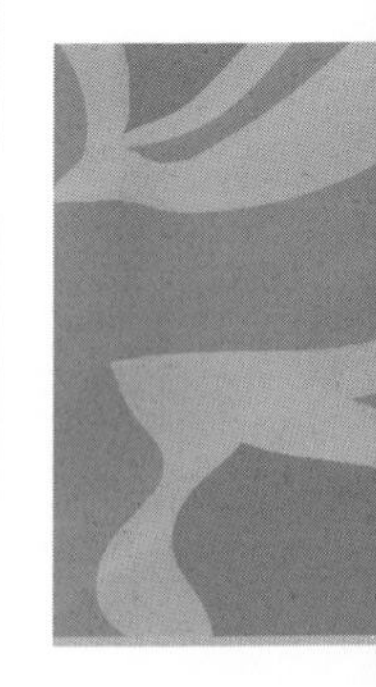

What next?

Read: David Tuck's article 'Paternalism and conservatism' in *Politics Review*, Vol. 31, No. 2, November 2021

Watch: 'One Nation Conservatism: what does it look like after COVID 19?' (16 November 2020), **https://policyexchange.org.uk**

Chapter 5

The constitution: the Johnsonian constitution 'in flux'

Focus

Students must have strong knowledge and understanding of the nature and sources of the UK constitution as well as all the major constitutional changes that have taken place since 1997. In addition, there is a requirement for students to evaluate the issues and debates around recent constitutional changes and whether constitutional reforms that have taken place should be taken further.

Edexcel	UK Government 1.4	Debates on further constitutional reform
AQA	3.1.1.1	Issues and debates around recent constitutional changes

Context

Boris Johnson's relatively short tenure at Number 10 has been accompanied by one of the most constitutionally turbulent periods in modern British history. However, while the late 1990s saw the introduction of far-reaching constitutional changes affecting all institutions of government and the United Kingdom as a whole, the coherence behind the reforms that took place under Tony Blair's New Labour a quarter of a century ago appears to many to be entirely lacking from the current changes.

That said, there are several discernible, though contentious, themes that run through the constitutional proposals and changes that have been proposed or enacted in recent years. For many commentators, the termination of the Fixed-term Parliaments Act (see page 35) signifies an aspiration to restore traditional prerogative powers to the executive; recent legal reviews have suggested refinements to the scope of judicial review and a rebalancing of the seemingly growing role of judges in political life; and the enduring presence of sometimes impenetrable 'conventions' within the UK's uncodified constitution have prompted calls for reform.

Box 5.1 Key definition

Constitutional reform: changes in the body of laws, rules and practices that govern how states function and how their political systems work. The UK's uncodified constitutional arrangements have permitted a host of changes that have affected areas such as the composition of parliament (the removal of most hereditary peers), the functioning of the judicial system (with the creation of the UK Supreme Court) and the relationships between nations in the union.

Why is the UK constitution described as being 'in flux'?

In recent years there has been a raft of political events, challenges and incidents that have shifted the UK's constitutional framework faster and further than at any previous time. Such events have included:

- Brexit and the implications for Northern Ireland's relationship with the rest of the United Kingdom
- the prorogation of parliament in 2019, when Boris Johnson suspended parliament for up to 5 weeks, and the subsequent Supreme Court challenge to the prime minister's use of prerogative powers
- recent independent reviews — into Administrative Law and Human Rights — that look set to shape future constitutional changes relating to the protection of rights
- proposals to restrict the scrutiny powers of the senior judiciary through legislation such as the UK Internal Market Bill which prevented them declaring parliamentary laws incompatible with EU law
- the repeal of the Fixed-term Parliaments Act to return the calling of general elections to the prime minister's prerogative powers
- the coronavirus health crisis that necessitated three lockdowns and a re-evaluation of the extent of emergency powers wielded by the state
- pressure on devolved arrangements, driven by support for the Scottish National Party and by developments in English devolution
- escalating tension between the government and the civil service leading to multiple resignations of permanent secretaries in 2020 and 2021, including permanent secretaries in the Home Office, Treasury and Justice Department

Taken together, such changes have given rise to the view that the UK's traditional constitutional strengths of flexibility and a lack of codified rigidity are hampering the effective and successful functioning of the state. Recently, calls from politicians and commentators have increased for a proper constitutional settlement for the United Kingdom.

What has been the impact of recent constitutional change?

Many of the recent constitutional changes — proposed and actual — may have had the appearance of disconnected or unrelated events, but they have nonetheless been underpinned by discernible themes. Individually and collectively, recent constitutional changes have made a substantial impact on key areas of political and institutional life, encompassing the enhancement of executive power, the reduction of judicial scrutiny and straining of constitutional conventions.

Enhancing executive power — the repeal of the Fixed-term Parliaments Act

In 2011, the coalition government passed the Fixed-term Parliaments Act (FTPA), which removed the prime minister's prerogative power to call a general election. The FTPA stipulated that general elections are to be held on a fixed-term basis every 5 years. General elections within 5 years are only permitted under exceptional circumstances and require a two-thirds parliamentary super-majority.

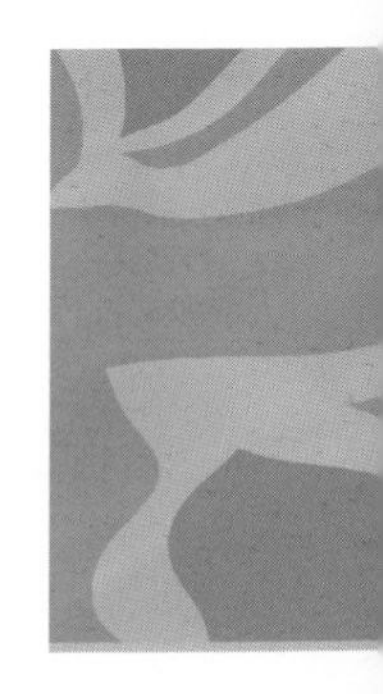

Box 5.2 Key definition

Prerogative power: the UK's constitutional arrangements retain a number of prerogative powers — those exercised formerly by the monarch but now by the executive, or prime minister, in the name of the monarch. Examples of prerogative powers exercised by the prime minister include the appointment and dismissal of ministers and, prior to the Fixed-term Parliaments Act, the dissolution of parliament.

Box 5.3 What was the Fixed-term Parliaments Act?

The Fixed-term Parliaments Act 2011 set a 5-year interval between ordinary general elections. The Act includes two mechanisms that could lead to early general elections. Early elections can be held only if:

- a motion for an early general election is agreed either by at least two-thirds of the whole House or without division, or
- a motion of no confidence is passed and no alternative government is confirmed by the Commons within 14 days

The Act put dissolution on a statutory footing. Previously, parliament had been dissolved by the queen, on the advice of the prime minister.

Adapted from the House of Commons Library

The Conservative government had long regarded the Act as unworkable and a recipe for 'paralysis', allowing ineffective governments, in the absence of two-thirds of the Commons supporting the calling of a general election, to continue in office for far longer than would formerly have been the case. In a bid to end the prospect of parliamentary 'delay and dither', an Act to repeal the FTPA returns the power to dissolve parliament and to call a general election to the prime minister. However, critics of the repeal of the FTPA have demanded alternative constitutional safeguards be put in place to guard against the arbitrary power of government to call general elections in times of crisis or emergency.

Reducing judicial scrutiny

Judicial review — the ability to challenge decisions made by public bodies — was the route by which two highly prominent court cases checked the government's authority during its handling of the UK's withdrawal from the EU.

- In 2017, in what *The Guardian* reported as 'one of the most significant constitutional decisions in a generation', the Supreme Court ruled that the government had to obtain parliament's authorisation before it could trigger article 50 to leave the EU.
- In 2019, the Supreme Court found that the prime minister's decision to prorogue parliament for 5 weeks, rather than the normal 4 to 5 days, in the midst of Brexit-related crisis talks, was 'unlawful'. There was widespread criticism that the prime minister's motivation was to stifle further parliamentary debate and scrutiny, and equivalent criticism of what was perceived as a 'political' decision when the Supreme Court quashed the prorogation.

Those Supreme Court decisions provided the basis for a Conservative Party 2019 manifesto commitment to ensure that the judicial review process was not abused 'to conduct politics by another means'.

In 2020, the government set up an Independent Review of Administrative Law (IRAL), looking into the law that governs the actions and decisions of public bodies. The IRAL reported in 2021 that certain types of judicial review, especially those with a low success rate, should be discontinued. The review also recommended that the Court's ability to 'give public bodies a time-limited opportunity to remedy an unlawful act instead of immediately striking it down' should be recognised in statute law.

Box 5.4 Judicial review success rate

In June 2021, the *New Law Journal* reported that the Office for Statistics Regulation (OSR) had backed a law firm's claim that the government 'had used overly simplified data in its submissions to the Independent Review of Administrative Law'. The IRAL had reported that in the 7 years between 2012 and 2019, just 12 (0.22%) of the more than 5,000 judicial reviews 'launched' within a particular category were successful.

While the lord chancellor, Robert Buckland, told parliament this was 'an astonishingly low rate', law firm Public Law Project (PLP) said that this was a 'poor conclusion' as the outcomes of many judicial review cases are successful but are not formally recorded as such because the success is not reached through the conclusion of a court process. A more accurate figure would be 12 successes out of 45 cases brought (representing a 26% success rate), since the results of only 45 cases were known at that time.

Source: *New Law Journal*, June 2021

Critics of the government's reforms to judicial review — including the Bar Council which represents 17,000 barristers — have raised concerns that the plans seek to limit the scope of judicial challenge and are impractical, with 'a lack of analysis of how the proposals would actually work'.

In addition, the government's appetite to reduce judicial scrutiny was revealed in the details of the recent UK Internal Market Bill. The power of the courts to identify and declare incompatible any 'subordinate legislation' (all 'legislation' below that of parliamentary statutes, such as food import and export regulations) which conflicts with non-UK law was reduced in extent by Clause 45 of the UK Internal Market Bill (as first introduced). This clause also compelled the courts to uphold subordinate legislation even if it conflicted with, for example, EU law. While the government pledged to 'deactivate' Clause 45 if a final deal with the EU was reached, it nevertheless permitted a breach of international law by seeking to change agreed import and export procedures for goods between Northern Ireland and the rest of the UK.

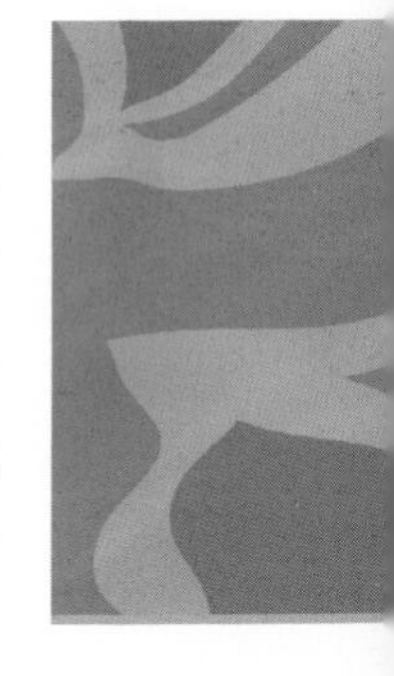

Stretching constitutional conventions

While the UK's constitution is uncodified, most of it is written down, though not in a single document. The 'unwritten' parts come in the form of constitutional conventions that play a key role in influencing important political processes and shaping relationships between institutions of state.

Box 5.5 Constitutional conventions

Constitutional conventions are often referred to as the 'unwritten' part of the UK's constitution and do not have the status of enforceable laws. Some conventions appear in written form, such as the Cabinet Manual and the Ministerial Code. Some are conceived at a specific moment to guide future behaviour, such as the Salisbury Convention, which governs the relationship between the Commons and Lords relating to manifesto commitments. Others evolve over time, like customs and traditions, and are rarely departed from without good reason. Further examples of constitutional conventions include traditions such as the prime minister being the leader of the largest party in the House of Commons, judges not playing an active part in political life, and ministers making themselves accountable to parliament.

In recent years there have been several occasions when 'unwritten' constitutional conventions have been strained, prompting calls for a full codification of the UK's constitutional arrangements.

The **Sewel convention** is an arrangement that regulates the relationship between the UK Parliament and the national assemblies of Scotland, Wales and Northern Ireland. It requires specific consent to be given from the devolved governments for any UK-wide legislation that encroaches on devolved matters, particularly health, legal and policing matters. If consent is refused, the UK Parliament can — and usually does — still pass the legislation, but reflecting ever-growing hostility, the three devolved governments now refuse this consent on multiple occasions each year. In addition:

- The passage of the UK Internal Market Act (2020) also saw substantial changes to the operation of devolved competences. When the Scottish Parliament and the Welsh Assembly withheld their legislative consent, the Act passed through the UK Parliament anyway.
- In September 2021 the Welsh Government refused to provide legislative consent for the UK Elections Bill that made photo identification compulsory when voting in general elections in Wales, yet the Act passed anyway.

Another constitutional convention is the expectation that the government and its ministers **behave responsibly** and **follow official advice**.

- In November 2020, Boris Johnson requested a review into his home secretary's conduct following allegations that Priti Patel had 'bullied' departmental staff. Independent adviser, Sir Alex Allan, found that the home secretary had indeed broken the Ministerial Code, most often by 'shouting and swearing' at

Whitehall officials. Despite the inquiry's findings, the prime minister took no further action.

- In December 2020, the House of Lords Appointments Commission refused to support the prime minister's intention to appoint Peter Cruddas to the House of Lords. The Commission advised that it was unable to support the nomination after carrying out its vetting. The prime minister made the appointment anyway.

Comparisons and connections

Perhaps the single most evident area of direct political comparison between the UK and USA lies in their constitutional frameworks. While there are certain similarities — in that they both seek to place democracy, rights, justice and the rule of law at the forefront — the differences are far more stark. Most recently:

- In **structural** terms, one of the most fundamental differences lies in the complete separation of powers dictated by the US constitution, compared to the fusion of the executive and legislature within the UK system. A UK prime minister with a sizeable Commons majority is often accused of being an 'elected dictator', able to push legislation through the chamber with relative ease. However, even a US president with a congressional majority in both houses — such as Trump between 2016 and 2018 — can find controlling the passage of legislation very difficult. In 2019, the Republican-controlled Senate blocked Trump-backed legislation related to the wall on the Mexican border.
- In **rational** terms, the 'policing' of the respective constitutions in the USA and UK has seen significant developments in recent years. There is little doubt that the US Supreme Court is substantially more powerful than the UK Supreme Court, with rulings that have had a wide-ranging impact on US politics and society. For example, landmark US Supreme Court rulings have checked presidential power for several centuries, while in the UK, recent Supreme Court rulings to check executive power were seen as ground-breaking, and led to sustained debate about the possible drift towards a constitutional court in the UK.
- In **cultural** terms, perhaps the most significant constitutional difference lies in the origins of the constitutional arrangements. While constitutional arrangements in the UK are the product of many centuries of evolutionary change incorporating sources such as the Magna Carta from the Middle Ages and parliamentary traditions that stretch back to Tudor times, the US constitution was codified at a fixed point and exhibits all the unique characteristics and preoccupations of its eighteenth-century origins — a fierce protection of religious freedom, individual rights and limited government.

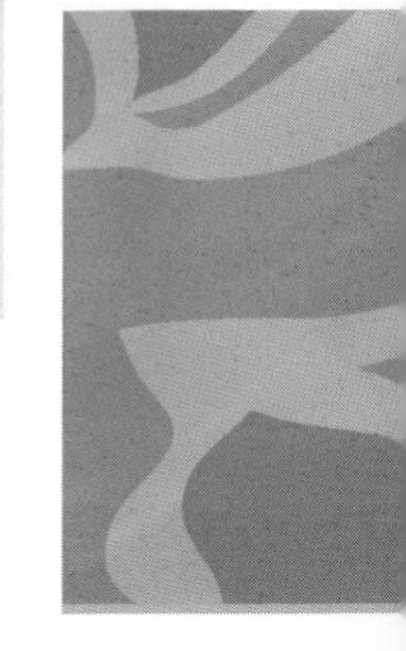

Exam success

Constitutional reform in the UK continues apace; sometimes planned, sometimes the product of unchecked events. One of the key areas of evaluation for students is whether the constitutional arrangements in the UK should be reformed to the extent of their codification in a final 'settlement'. Questions in this area may be framed as follows:

- *Evaluate the extent to which the UK should codify its constitution.* (Edexcel-style, 30 marks)
- *'The UK should codify its constitution.' Analyse and evaluate this statement.* (AQA-style, 25 marks)

Top-level responses will place the arguments for constitutional codification against a backdrop of recent changes, reviewing the extent to which the enhancement of executive power, the decline in judicial scrutiny and the straining of uncodified conventions have boosted the case for major change towards a constitutional settlement. Other evaluation will include:

- The balance between evolutionary flexibility and unhelpful ambiguity. Many commentators point to the post-referendum Brexit turmoil, which lasted for several years in the absence of a clear constitutional framework for resolving a referendum vote, as evidence of the need to codify arrangements.
- The importance of clarity over the protection of rights. The identification and entrenchment of civil rights is a key element of a codified document. The UK has long battled concerns over how to champion civil rights without diminishing parliamentary authority.
- The historic supremacy of parliament is a feature of UK politics that has stood the test of time and the settled mode of politics in the UK reflects the importance of consensus and restraint.

What next?

Read: the Ministerial Code investigation into the home secretary's conduct in government (**www.gov.uk/government/news/ministerial-code-investigation**)

Chapter 6

Devolution (Part 1): what is the future for English representation in Westminster?

Focus

Examination specifications focus on the role and powers of all the devolved bodies in the UK, and the impact of the process of devolution on government and politics in the UK. In addition, the focus is also upon devolution in England, how questions over English governance should be resolved, and the future of English representation in Westminster.

Edexcel	UK Government 1.3	The impact of devolution on the UK
AQA	3.1.1.5	The impact of devolution on government in the UK

Context

The UK Parliament's Public Administration and Constitutional Affairs Committee (PACAC) explains devolution as having become an 'established part of the UK constitutional architecture'. Yet while legislative and executive devolution has been instituted and developed in all non-English national regions of the UK — Scotland, Wales and Northern Ireland — and although procedures passed in 2015 did allow for English-only MPs in the UK Parliament to vote exclusively on laws deemed only to affect England, there has been no similar level of devolution in England.

The early 2020s have seen developments in all aspects of the central questions relating to how a post-devolution England should be governed. In particular for students of politics, the issue of non-English MPs able to influence UK parliamentary legislation that affects England alone is a controversy that has reawakened after parliamentary procedures known as English votes for English laws (EVEL) were abolished in 2021.

Two key areas of understanding, analysis and evaluation are:

1. The political issues around EVEL, and the reasons for its introduction in 2015 and its abolition in 2021.
2. The consequences of the abolition of EVEL and the implications for English representation in Westminster.

Box 6.1 English votes for English laws (EVEL)

In the 2000s, legislation that affected England alone was passed by the Labour government in the UK Parliament with decisive support from MPs who represented non-English constituencies. This issue became a long-standing grievance for the then Conservative opposition, which commissioned a report in 2008 that proposed restricting the participation of MPs representing non-English constituencies during the passage of bills relating only to England.

What happened to 'English votes for English laws'?

In 2021, UK parliamentary procedures known as English votes for English laws (EVEL) were abolished. EVEL was introduced in 2015 in response to concerns that non-English MPs were able to influence legislation that did not affect their constituencies, particularly relating to the devolved matters of health and education.

Box 6.2 The introduction and abolition of EVEL

The 2015 Conservative election manifesto included a proposal that England-only legislation should be subject to different procedures, with Westminster MPs from Northern Ireland, Scotland and Wales unable to vote on matters that affected only England — just as MPs from England were unable to vote on matters devolved to the Northern Ireland Assembly, the Scottish Parliament and the Welsh Senedd.

English votes for English laws procedures (or 'standing orders') were adopted in 2015, suspended in April 2020 to streamline parliamentary procedures during the Covid-19 pandemic, and finally abolished in July 2021

From the outset there was resistance to the introduction of EVEL procedures. Arguments against them included the following:

1. Historically, the Scottish National Party (SNP) had customarily not voted on England-only legislation, but EVEL formalised that custom into law. The new procedures were controversial in that they effectively created two classes of MPs at Westminster, with some representatives prohibited from engaging with certain types of legislation.
2. While certain matters considered by the UK Parliament may have affected England alone, public spending commitments, for example on reforming and modernising health and social care in England, could well have had a much wider or adverse impact on the capacity of public spending in the whole of the UK. Defining an 'England-only law' is notoriously difficult.
3. Less than a third of governments since 1945 have enjoyed support from a sufficient number of England-only MPs to form an 'English majority'. EVEL procedures would bar many governments from enacting manifesto commitments related to important areas, such as health and education.

Why was EVEL abolished?

To many onlookers, the decision to abolish EVEL runs counter to the sentiments of a government that makes much of its support for causes that affect English voters. However, just like other significant constitutional changes, a single vote by the Conservative majority government in the House of Commons is all that is required to make what amounts to an important change for the UK.

Box 6.3 Deliver us from EVEL?

UCL's Constitution Unit explained in July 2021 that the government's abolition stance can be partly explained by a number of inter-related factors. These include:

- the enthusiasm of the current Conservative government to distance itself from the perceived failures of recent Tory administrations, especially the legacy of the Cameron/coalition government
- a reckoning that anything leading to upset among SNP MPs in parliament should be avoided, in a bid to better manage Scotland's relationship with the Union
- a more sympathetic understanding of the issues thrown up by preventing Scottish MPs from voting on matters that might indirectly affect their constituents, for example affecting the 'Barnett formula'
- undermining the future possibility of an MP representing a Scottish constituency one day becoming prime minister

However, the complaint that the 'unduly complex and opaque' nature of EVEL procedures has generated a significant amount of administrative work is perhaps seen as the single biggest factor in its demise. As the Constitution Unit reveals:

> The procedures have generated a substantial amount of administrative work for Commons officials, enabling the Speaker since 2015 to certify parts of 51 bills and 237 statutory instruments. They have also created considerable disruption to Commons proceedings. EVEL comprises a complex set of rules that are little understood, or even noticed, by many MPs and close observers of Westminster. Its arcane and restricted character means that EVEL was never going to be a meaningful answer to the much wider question about English feelings towards the Union raised by Cameron in the aftermath of the 2014 Scottish independence referendum.

Adapted from 'Deliver us from EVEL? Is the government right to abolish "English Votes for English Laws"?', The Constitution Unit, June 2021

In July 2021, the leader of the House of Commons, Jacob Rees-Mogg, countered accusations that the abolition of EVEL was designed to appease the SNP, instead focusing on the 'confidence' that the government had in 'our Union parliament'.

However, the SNP had long campaigned against EVEL and in February 2020 SNP MPs had led a Commons protest — disrupting one of the voting lobbies — after they were prevented from voting on the NHS Funding Bill which, they claimed, would ultimately affect how much was spent in Scotland through the

Barnett formula (the formula devised to fund devolved matters in Scotland). Consequently, the demise of EVEL led the SNP's Peter Wishart, shadow leader of the House of Commons and chair of the Scottish Affairs Select Committee, to label the abolition 'an utter, utter humiliation' for the UK government and a 'spectacular victory' for the SNP.

Box 6.4 Contrasting views on the decision to abolish the English votes for English laws procedure

It is not just the ability of [the House of Commons] to legislate effectively that has been constrained, more fundamentally, the EVEL procedure has also undermined the role of this parliament as the Union parliament in which all parts of the United Kingdom are represented equally. There should be an equal representation of all members.

Jacob Rees-Mogg, July 2021

A flagship policy of the 2015 manifesto will soon be nothing more than a footnote in future constitutional history books and remembered as just another Tory policy disaster. They were consumed with the notion that we, the unkempt Caledonian hoards, were somehow stopping them securing the democratic outcomes that they desired. That us Scots MPs...needed to be constrained and needed to be curtailed. EVEL was just about the worst solution to a problem that didn't even exist.

Peter Wishart, July 2021

Post-EVEL: what does the future hold for English representation in Westminster?

For many, the abolition of EVEL has undermined any sense — real or perceived — that the future of England in a post-devolved UK is a matter taken 'seriously' by the current Conservative government. If the main driving force for EVEL's introduction was the development of a confident, distinctive and more assertive English 'voice' in Westminster, its removal, without a clear alternative, re-opens some of the biggest questions about England's future within the union.

That said, EVEL came well short on delivering its central objective. Hopes for this 'confident and more assertive' English voice lay in large part in a principal element of the EVEL procedures — that of the setup of a special 'legislative grand committee' to follow a designated bill's report stage. This phase, for 'English-only' bills, was introduced to permit English (or English and Welsh) MPs to deliberate and then signify their 'consent' in a symbolic extra legislative stage.

However, up to EVEL's abolition, this new 'legislative grand committee' stage occurred just 42 times and, as UCL's Constitution Unit research shows, 'only in four cases did they last longer than 10 minutes'. UCL's conclusion is that in this and other ways, EVEL fell 'a long way short of providing meaningful opportunities for deliberation over, or the articulation of, English interests'.

Enacting then abolishing EVEL within a matter of a few years reflects the fact that many intended 'solutions' to the problem of how England should be governed lack cross-party support and appear to create further problems.

The abolition of EVEL has, however, permitted the possibility that other, more suitable ways of promoting and protecting the interests of England in parliament can be considered. Two alternatives include:

1 As a substitute for EVEL and prior to its introduction, the McKay Commission proposed a number of alternatives in its report 'Commission on the consequences of devolution for the House of Commons' in 2013. One option, which gathered cross-party support and was far simpler than EVEL, proposed a non-binding stage at the start of a designed bill's legislative journey, during which the preferences and interests of English-only MPs could be articulated and made known.

2 As a broader alternative to EVEL, UCL's Constitution Unit has long argued for a new 'English Affairs select committee' with a wide remit, modelled partly on the existing committees for Scottish, Welsh and Northern Ireland Affairs. A primary role of the committee would be to highlight concerns about England-only legislation for the attention of the Commons.

Box 6.5 The McKay Commission, 2013

The findings and proposals of the McKay Commission for a post-devolved England have seen a revival in the early 2020s. Nearly a decade ago, the Commission chaired by Sir William McKay reviewed the impact on the procedures in the House of Commons of legislation that affected only certain parts of the UK.

Its main recommendation — that future legislation affecting England but not other parts of the UK should require the support of a majority of MPs sitting for English constituencies — was developed into EVEL, but a range of procedural changes were suggested to allow the English voice to be heard. These included committees on English-only bills that reflected English party balance, motions on the floor of the House to permit English-only MPs to have their say and the creation of a 'select committee on devolution' to better scrutinise the impact of devolution on existing procedures.

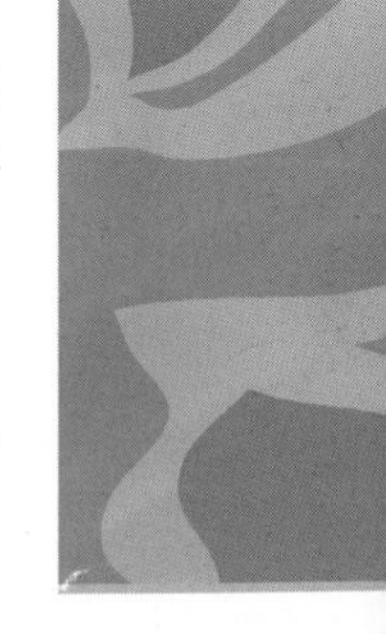

Ultimately, while EVEL procedures were complicated, time consuming and failed to fully deliver the expected elevation of England's 'voice', they did at least attempt to tackle the possibility of a future legitimacy crisis in the UK Parliament. The possibility of a future British government propped up by non-English MPs (for example even a loose coalition of Labour and the Scottish National Party) could find itself at odds with an English majority in Westminster when it comes to legislation on important devolved matters.

Comparisons and connections

Debates over the legislative relationships between the constituent parts of the UK, especially the autonomy and authority of England, lead to one of the most common comparisons made between governing arrangements in the UK and USA. While there are certain similarities between devolution in the UK and federalism in the USA since both see powers and responsibilities exercised at governing levels 'below' the centre, the differences between devolution in the UK and federalism in the USA are far more significant than the similarities.

- In the USA's federal system, **every state possesses the same powers** regardless of population or geographic size, whereas the UK's regions all have different powers. For example, the Scottish Parliament can vary tax rates (within 3% of the UK income tax rate) while the Welsh Assembly cannot.
- In the USA **state powers are entrenched and constitutionally enumerated** so cannot be removed or varied except by constitutional change. In the UK, devolved powers are exercised only by Act of Parliament and can be varied by further Acts (such as the Scotland Act, 2016, which devolved a number of transport and finance-related powers) or withdrawn if devolved responsibilities cannot be met (such as when Northern Ireland's Assembly was suspended recently between 2017 and 2020).
- In the USA, **state powers are said to have diminished over time**, as the federal government becomes more involved with USA-wide initiatives in healthcare, especially evidenced in the Covid-19 vaccine rollout programme in 2021, and education. On the other hand, devolved powers in the UK have grown relentlessly over the last 25 years with powers, such as those over local taxation regimes, being handed to Scottish and Welsh national assemblies, and to metro-mayors in England.

What next?

Read: Dan Taborda's article 'Edexcel 12-mark comparative questions' in *Politics Review,* Volume 31, Issue 2, which focuses on the differences between devolution and federalism

Research: The Constitution Unit's 'Deliver us from EVEL? Is the government right to abolish "English Votes for English Laws"?', **https://constitution-unit.com**

Chapter 7

Devolution (Part 2): what does the government's 'levelling up' agenda mean for devolved government in England?

Focus

Examination specifications focus on the role and powers of all the devolved bodies in the UK, and the impact of the process of devolution on government and politics in the UK. In addition, the focus is also upon devolution in England, how questions over English governance should be resolved, and the extent to which devolved government should be extended in England.

Edexcel	UK Government 1.3	The impact of devolution on the UK
AQA	3.1.1.5	The impact of devolution on government in the UK

Context

Alongside a strengthening of the Scottish independence cause has come a growing public and political view that England ought to be served much better by the UK's devolved arrangements. Accusations from the Scottish National Party (SNP) that the UK Parliament looks after the interests of England above those of the Union — hence the SNP reference to an English Parliament 'squatting' in the national parliament — have been matched by a rise in 'English separatism' to potentially provide a basis for an English national parliament.

The early 2020s have seen developments in all aspects of the central questions relating to how a post-devolution England should be governed. This 'English question' remains as controversial and relevant to students of politics as ever and includes:

- The devolution of power to English cities and regions in bespoke deals has led to what some consider to be an unsustainable mix of different governing models and regional powers. Questions remain over the extent to which the government's 'levelling up' agenda will genuinely empower English regions.
- Magnified by governing difficulties during the health pandemic is a growing belief that England could be served better — and that the creation of an English national parliament within a federal UK could well be the logical direction of post-devolution UK.

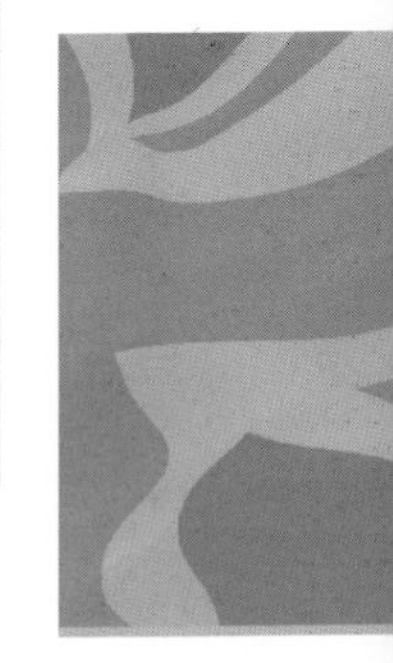

Box 7.1 Key definition

Levelling up: despite using the term many times, the UK government has often been accused of not defining what it means. The Centre for Cities (**www.centreforcities.org**) defines levelling up as narrowing the divergence seen across the country in areas such as health, education and public service provision, and ensuring that every area within the UK reaches its productivity potential.

Will the government's 'levelling up' agenda revive plans for regional government in England?

Proposals for regional government within England have long been part of plans to create a more balanced devolved settlement for England within the UK. However, such plans have often struggled against the lack of deep-rooted regional identity felt within England: while many people may identify with their immediate locality, city or county, few people have strong feelings for large regional areas such as the East Midlands or the North West.

In response to this, Boris Johnson outlined a vision for the UK that placed greater devolution of power at its heart. In a speech in Coventry in July 2021, the prime minister committed to 'rewriting the rule book' with 'a more flexible approach to devolution' in England. Rather than focus on regions, Johnson explained that 'there is no reason why our great counties cannot benefit from the same powers we have devolved to city leaders'.

Some critics of Boris Johnson's vision for the UK cite the 'State of the North' report recently published by the Institute for Public Policy (IPPR) which reveals that the UK is one of the most regionally divided countries in the developed world — with little sign that governing changes will improve things.

Box 7.2 English devolution

Although some powers have been passed down from central government, they often come with limitations on their use and, with some exceptions, do not include the power to raise revenue. The majority of funding continues to come from central grants that can be withdrawn/modified at ministerial discretion. And recent spats with the likes of Andy Burnham [Mayor of Greater Manchester] have reminded ministers of the political dangers of creating regional power bases. The result is that local government in England is now a surely unsustainable patchwork of different governance models and powers. Whitehall retains tight control.

David Higham, on The Constitution Society website (https://consoc.org.uk), 30 January 2021

Many in the North point to growing unemployment and the lowering of wages and life expectancy, claiming that the 'continued overcentralisation of power and resources in Whitehall is the root cause of this'.

Box 7.3 Levelling up should radically re-imagine how regions across England are empowered

The good news is that the bold ideas needed already exist. Evidence shows devolution can help to deliver better policy for places. And, in a speech otherwise low on solutions, the Prime Minister did recognise this. He acknowledged devolution's role in reducing inequalities between East and West Germany, now smaller than the UK's own divides. Yet, he is missing something crucial: the German system is built on high levels of decentralisation, large state investment, a role for regional leaders within central government, and large fiscal transfers between states. To achieve anything like that success, English devolution must be far more expansive and resources much larger.

Marcus Johns on the Politics Home website (www.politicshome.com), 20 July 2021

Regional disparities in the UK are as increasingly prominent as they are stark. In October 2021 a new government Office for Health Improvement and Disparities (OHID) was launched 'to help people live longer, healthier and happier lives'. Amongst many challenges, the new Office aims to tackle health disparities across the UK 'which mean men in the most deprived areas in England are expected to live nearly 10 years fewer than those in the least deprived'.

Box 7.4 Challenges for the Office for Health Improvement and Disparities (OHID)

The latest figures show clear trends, based on geographical location, of a person's life expectancy and the years they can expect to live a healthy life. For example:

- Men in the most deprived areas in England are expected to live nearly 10 years fewer than those in the least deprived. Women in the same areas can expect to live 7 years fewer.
- Smoking is more prevalent in more deprived areas and one of the leading causes of inequalities in life expectancy; an international study found it accounts for half the difference in mortality between the least and most deprived men aged 35 to 69.
- Obesity is widespread but more prevalent among the most deprived areas; prevalence is almost 8% higher among those living in the most deprived decile of local authorities (66.6%) compared to those in the least deprived areas (58.8%).

Adapted from the Office for Health Improvement and Disparities, www.gov.uk

However, there remain many concerns about how cities or regions across England can be empowered through a process of devolution:

- Will the UK government ever commit to such an extensive project of decentralising power? To genuinely 'level up' and create institutions across England that possess London-style powers is a complex undertaking that will take many years to deliver.
- The basis for a regional England has yet to establish any sort of consensus. Some argue for an England based on a metro-mayor model: elected leaders with wide-ranging powers and resources to develop larger regions. Others see the strengthening of local government as the key to the advancement of

smaller communities: bringing decision-making on housing, transport and skills development closer to the people.
- While all major UK parties support the devolution of some governing functions to city regions or to combined authorities, the desirability of English regional bodies possessing law-making powers — meaning that regions could steadily deviate from one another — is contested.

In a variation to this, and responding to the lack of English representation to replicate that of other national regions, the *Financial Times'* Whitehall editor argued in September 2021 that the House of Lords — a 'bloated unelected chamber with 820 members...well past its sell-by date' — should be abolished and replaced with a new chamber of 200 'legislative experts' from all regions of the UK. Weaving together the lack of English 'voice' and regional disparities, Sebastian Payne asserted that 'tackling regional inequality can only be done by tackling England's democratic deficit'. And bringing representatives from the Welsh Assembly, Scottish Parliament, Northern Irish Assembly and England's mayoral regions 'into the heart of national politics...could help secure the future of the United Kingdom too'.

Why doesn't England have a national parliament?

For some, the issues relating to English regional inequality and the absence of a confident voice to challenge the status quo and champion a response will be resolved only if English issues are represented more effectively within a national assembly.

However, the original devolution settlement introduced as part of New Labour's wide-ranging programme of constitutional reforms in the 1990s did not include proposals for an English national assembly or national parliament. Factors that explain England's divergence from other UK regions in this respect include:

- With the UK Parliament based in London, and alongside the disproportionate size and influence of England within the Union, an English Parliament was seen as likely to challenge the power and authority of the UK Parliament, potentially destabilising the political union of the UK. Votes in a UK Parliament, if representative of the UK, could be frequently manipulated to support the view of an English assembly.
- Proposals for devolving power within England centred instead upon making London responsible for a greater number of policy areas that affected the capital, especially transport, through the creation of a directly elected mayor and a Greater London Assembly (GLA).
- With around 85% of the UK's population living in England, plans also focused on enhancing English regional responsibilities, for which there appeared to be substantially more support than for the creation of an English national assembly. However, English regional plans were abandoned after 78% of voters in the northeast opposed their creation in a referendum.

- Plans for devolution in England were clearly different to those of other regions of the UK, but devolution differed substantially within all regions of the UK anyway. The Scottish Parliament has tax-varying powers and the ability to pass primary legislation in a number of defined areas. While the Welsh Assembly originally had no power to pass its own primary legislation, it now does in several areas such as energy, transport and employment. Northern Ireland's devolved arrangements were inseparable from the peace process with specific cross-party power-sharing requirements.

Enthusiasm for an English national parliament or assembly appeared to hit new heights in the wake of the Scottish independence referendum. In 2018, the BBC reported that 'calls for the creation an English Parliament reached a crescendo' in the referendum's immediate aftermath 'when more powers were promised for the Scottish Parliament'. However, the report went on to explain that 'the clamour has died down for now', after the Brexit result was felt to have given voice to a tide of English nationalism.

Box 7.5 England 'denied a voice'

Devolution to Scotland and Wales but not to England means Scottish, Welsh and Northern Irish voters decide the government of England. If one day we end up with a UK government elected with no English majority, but expected to determine policies in England that are devolved elsewhere, we will face a constitutional crisis. The only sustainable remaining solution is an English parliament and English government within a federal UK, supported by a political culture that respects and cherishes pride in England and shows a more serious commitment to the government of England's regions.

Nick Timothy in the *Daily Telegraph*, 4 July 2021

Nevertheless, the early 2020s have seen a steadily growing body of opinion argue that England should indeed be given its own parliament. According to Nick Timothy, Downing Street chief of staff under Theresa May, England does indeed have its own 'identity' that would benefit from being recognised with the 'democratic, institutional and political voice the English deserve'.

Arguments in favour of the creation of an English Parliament stress the representative possibilities of an institution located away from London, alongside a process of democratic renewal and modernisation, with the abolition of the House of Lords and a fully federal UK — dealing mainly with foreign affairs and macro-economic policy — beneath a codified constitutional settlement.

On the other hand, arguments against the creation of an English Parliament focus on the insurmountable difficulties posed by a heavily imbalanced federal system that contains one very large member state and several much smaller ones; the cost and inefficiencies of multiple tiers of government, and a magnification rather than a reduction of the conflict between constituent parts of the UK.

Exam success

Devolution in the UK is an on-going, dynamic process with powers and responsibilities being decentralised at varying rates and in response to often conflicting demands. However, one of the most evident disparities in a devolved UK is the imbalance that exists between national regions, with England lacking a national assembly or parliament. Questions in this area may be framed as follows:

- *Evaluate the extent to which devolution in the UK should extend to the creation of an English national parliament.* (Edexcel-style, 30 marks)
- *'England should have its own national parliament.' Analyse and evaluate this statement.* (AQA-style, 25 marks)

The best responses will place the arguments for a devolved national parliament in England in context with the wider process of devolution in the UK nations, and also the wider arguments — such as English Votes for English Laws and English regional government — over how England should be governed.

- The most substantial argument in favour of the creation of an English Parliament is that, for many, it is the only effective way of **completing the process of devolution in the UK** and of resolving the questions about how England should be governed. However, its creation would inevitably lead to tension between the authority and jurisdiction of a UK Parliament and that of an English Parliament.
- The lack of **political recognition of an English identity** is likely to fester unresolved until provided with a democratic and institutional voice. There is little doubt that the creation of national bodies in Scotland and Wales have advanced Scottish and Welsh interests and identities respectively. That said, such unusual size and population imbalances between national territories within a federal structure are likely to pose severe challenges.
- The **creation of an effective federal structure** may well allow for the preservation of an historic union of nations with the UK Parliament focused upon federal issues — particularly economic and foreign affairs — and with all domestic matters devolved to national governments. However, while recent polling data indicates a rise in support for an English Parliament, support for retaining the status quo still far outstrips it.
- The argument also encompasses the prospect of **the UK becoming a federal state**. While settling on a federal structure could provide coherence and clarity, the dominance of England and the likely disputes over jurisdiction, funding, cross-national infrastructure and differing aims could well prove to be distracting at a time of global complexity.

What next?

Watch: The Constitution Unit (UCL) short video *Jack Sheldon: Options for an English Parliament*, **www.ucl.ac.uk/constitution-unit**

Watch: The Institute for Government's video: *What does 'levelling up' really mean? How to turn a promise into reality'*, **www.instituteforgovernment.org.uk**

Read: about the role and responsibilities of the government's Office for Health Improvement and Disparities in 'New era of public health to tackle inequalities and level up the UK', **www.gov.uk**

Chapter 8

Parliament and the executive: the changing relationship between parliament and the executive in the 2020s

Focus

The examination specifications require effective knowledge of the ways that parliament scrutinises government and executive activity and how the relationship between these two branches of government is changing. The most prominent forms of scrutiny take place on the floor of the House, through questions from the Opposition, and in Prime Minister's Questions. In addition, a sustained growth in the appetite of select committee to probe into uncomfortable areas of government life provides further areas of analysis of the relationship between parliament and the executive.

Edexcel	UK Government 2.1–2.4 and 4.2	Including: the main functions of the Commons and the ways in which parliament interacts with the executive
AQA	3.1.1.2 and 3.1.1.3	Including: scrutiny of the executive and the interaction of parliament with other branches of government

Context

The protracted Brexit process and questions over government accountability during the Covid health crisis have prompted many to review and question afresh the effectiveness of parliamentary scrutiny in the UK. The absence of a codified constitution to clearly set out parliament's responsibilities, the lack of full separation between executive and legislature, which permits the executive to dominate, and the use of a majoritarian electoral system to regularly deliver disproportionately large governing majorities all point to the inherent weakness of the procedures and protocols that guide parliament's scrutiny function.

There is little doubt that the online nature of parliamentary scrutiny during lockdown phases of the health crisis diminished the effectiveness of parliament's most vital function. Students of politics need up-to-date examples to enhance evaluation and analysis of the changing nature of parliament–executive relations. While a full review of the impact of the health crisis on the relationship between parliament and the executive is given in Chapter 8 of the 2021 Annual Update, this chapter focuses on contemporary

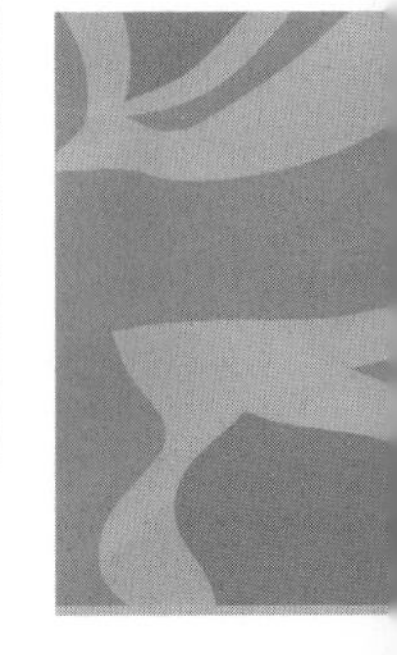

examples in the post-Brexit, post-pandemic period of the scrutiny role that parliament plays, in particular:

- the continued significance of Prime Minister's Questions, now in its sixtieth year in the current format, and the role of the leader of the opposition
- the importance of select committee activity in scrutinising the performance of the government and government decision-making during the health crisis and in other matters
- the role of backbenchers in checking the power of the government and representing constituents effectively

Box 8.1 Key definitions

Prime Minister's Questions (PMQs): takes place every Wednesday at midday when parliament is in session and lasts for half-an-hour. First introduced by Harold Macmillan in 1961, PMQs is one of the most visible examples of the legislature holding the executive to account.

Select committees: parliamentary committees that play important scrutiny roles in the Commons and the Lords. Their role is to examine the government by investigating its policies, performance and behaviours. Some of the most notable committees — such as the Public Accounts Committee and the Liaison Committee, which is made up of the chairs of all committees — are particularly influential.

The opposition: all parties that hold seats in the Commons other than the party of government. The official opposition is the next largest party to the governing party, and, together with its leader, takes on formal responsibilities and roles to challenge the government and present a viable alternative government in the run-up to general elections.

Sixty years of Prime Minister's Questions

Prime Minister's Questions (PMQs) pits the PM of the day primarily against the leader of the opposition, but also against the whole House, and is broadcast live before the wider viewing public. It is often a spectacle to behold, lionised by many around the world as 'adversarial politics' at its very best.

PMQs had its 60th anniversary in the current, modern format in July 2021, and it is an event that remains a real test for any prime minister. Sir Anthony Seldon, biographer of all prime ministers from John Major to Theresa May, reveals that PMQs 'take hours of preparation, and many prime ministers find them to be the most stressful part of the entire job'. At stake is the credibility and authority of the prime minister and invaluable opportunities for the leader of the opposition to dictate the political agenda. 'If the PM fails to impress,' asserts Seldon, 'as Brown and May did, morale on their own side declines, while the confidence of the opposition grows.'

In 2021, several notable exchanges during PMQs shaped the political agenda in the weeks to come:

- In March 2021, pay rises for NHS staff dominated the political agenda. On 10 March, Keir Starmer attacked the prime minister over the government's proposed 1% rise. 'They can afford to give Dominic Cummings a 40% pay rise,' said Starmer, 'but they can't afford to reward the NHS properly.' And 'even his own MPs know he's got this wrong'. The exchange kept the issue in the spotlight and 4 months later in July 2021 the government announced a 3% pay rise for NHS staff.
- In June 2021, Keir Starmer accused Boris Johnson of 'squandering' the successful Covid vaccine rollout when he 'let the Delta variant take hold' by delaying the blocking of arrivals from India. India was not placed on the UK's border-controlled 'red list' until 23 April, despite evidence of a highly transmissible variant many weeks before that, permitting up to 20,000 people to arrive through the delay. 'What on earth did the prime minister expect to be the consequences of that?' Starmer demanded. The prominence of the issue at PMQs kept alive a direct link between alleged government 'inaction' and the postponement of an ensuing stage of Covid reopening in July, further eroding the credibility of the government's handling of the health crisis.
- In September 2021, Boris Johnson was accused of 'hammering' workers and 'making a bad situation worse' by ending the Universal Credit uplift and raising national insurance. Keir Starmer used PMQs to expose divisions within the Conservative Party and to challenge the prime minister on the accuracy of statements from the work and pensions secretary, Thérèse Coffey, who claimed that workers would only have to work an extra 2 hours to make up the difference.

While Prime Minister's Questions can affect the authority of the party leaders, and at times shape the political agenda, the impact of PMQs on public perceptions of the effectiveness of the parliamentary scrutiny role is not easy to quantify. In 2021 the *Journal of Legislative Studies* published a wide-ranging study on 'the effect of Prime Minister's Questions on citizen efficacy and trust in parliament'. The study described PMQs as 'the most viewed and commented upon part of the parliamentary week' but one that 'attracts strong criticism as a noisy charade promoting a poor image of politics'. It also revealed that 'contrary to its negative reputation, PMQs does not adversely affect most citizens' perceptions,' who see in the robustness of the debate and the directness of the parliamentary process an appropriate symbol of healthy parliamentary democracy.

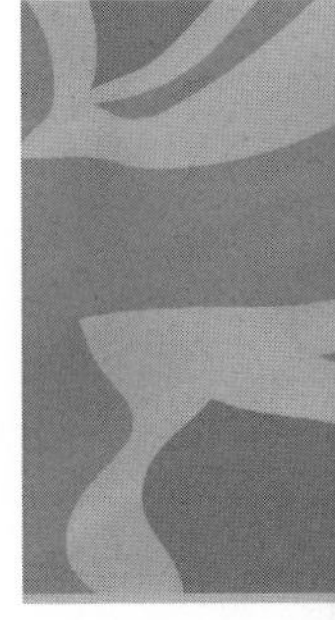

Pandemic and post-Brexit select committee activity

The Covid-19 health crisis and the government's response to it dominated much of the work of parliamentary select committees in the 2019–21 session. According to the Institute for Government — an independent think tank advocating reforms to government — at a time when a 'virtual' parliament struggled to scrutinise Covid legislation and other government activity, 'committees were able to push ministers and officials for more details on the evidence underpinning their decisions and ask questions of the government's pandemic response', meaning that the executive accountability 'gap' was at least partly filled by vital work done by select committees.

Almost every committee held at least one Covid-related inquiry in the 2019–21 session, and some committees devoted significant amounts of time to it.

Box 8.2 Pandemic-related select committee activity

According to the Institute for Government, the Women and Equalities Committee had the highest proportion of Covid-related inquiries (6 of 12, 50%), driven by 'four inquiries focused on the unequal impact of the pandemic on groups with protected characteristics — an area of particular concern during Covid'. The Health and Social Care Committee had the second highest proportion of inquiries related to Covid (4 of 11, 36%). These ranged from inquiries into the short-term response to the pandemic to the longer-term implications for the NHS.

Adapted from the Institute for Government, Parliamentary Monitor 2021

In addition, several significant changes in select committee composition and activity in both the Commons and the Lords have occurred, including:

- A continued growth in the number of committee chairs with recent ministerial experience, such as Jeremy Hunt (former health secretary and chair of the Health and Social Care Select Committee) and Yvette Cooper (a Labour government minister under Blair and Brown and chair of the Home Affairs Select Committee), is perceived to be a factor in their growing profile.
- The move to virtual proceedings enabled many committees to take evidence from a much wider pool of witnesses. According to the Institute for Government's report, 'virtual proceedings...made it easier for those from outside London, and with other commitments such as childcare, to attend oral evidence sessions'. In addition, witnesses assisted the committees by giving evidence 'quickly and easily' from 'Afghanistan, the US, Taiwan, Japan, South Korea, Hong Kong, Germany and Austria'.
- The post-Brexit and EU transition period has also had an impact on the structure of select committees in the Commons and the Lords, with new committees created, and others retired or reformed as the end of EU law in the UK changed the scrutiny needs of the UK Parliament. In the House of Lords, the European Union Select Committee, an expert legal body that had been responsible for scrutinising EU proposals and documents, was 'retired'.

Case study: Dominic Cummings gives select committee evidence

In March 2021, Boris Johnson's former top adviser was summoned and gave evidence to a joint session of the Commons Health and Science and Technology select committees. Dominic Cummings was questioned on the government's decision-making and its handling of the health crisis. Cummings told the committee that there was 'no doubt' that many senior people had performed 'far, far disastrously below the standards which the country has a right to expect. I think the Secretary of State for Health is certainly one of those people.' Dominic Cummings said that he had repeatedly urged the prime minister to sack the health secretary in order to prevent 'another set of disasters in the autumn'.

The immediate response to Cummings's testimony from a Downing Street spokesman was to 'absolutely reject Mr Cummings' claims about the Health Secretary' and to insist that the health secretary had the prime minister's full support. Yet the select committee evidence gave a high-profile platform to Cummings's assertions and when the health secretary was revealed to have 'breached social distancing guidance' by kissing a colleague just a few months later, he was forced to resign.

However, criticisms remain that select committees, on the most important and sensitive matters, are largely 'toothless'. Some select committees vented their frustration when attempts to get the government to engage with them were rebuffed. The House of Lords Covid Committee took the 'unusual step' of publishing a report condemning the government's response to and engagement with its inquiry on parliament's hybrid working arrangements. According to the Institute for Government, 'the committee noted that the government had failed to respond to a third of its recommendations'.

Backbench pressure on the government

Backbench activity in the House of Commons is invariably subject to a 'numbers game' relating to the size of the government's majority. With an 80-seat margin since 2019, Boris Johnson can largely ignore all but the most sizeable of backbench threats. Nevertheless, on a number of notable occasions, the Conservative backbenchers proved to be sufficiently restless to threaten or extract concessions from the government:

- In January 2021, China's role in persecuting Uighur Muslims in Xinjiang led many Conservative backbenchers to support an opposition amendment to give the courts the power to assess cases of alleged genocide, potentially forcing the government to reconsider any trade deal with a country found by the high court to be committing genocide. The amendment was supported by religious groups and a powerful cross-party alliance of MPs but defeated by 319 to 308. The scare led the government to offer a series of concessions including strengthening the Foreign Affairs Select Committee's powers to investigate whether breaches of human rights should prevent the UK from negotiating a free trade deal.
- In June 2021, the *Financial Times* commented on the largest backbench rebellion related to Covid legislation as Conservative MPs opposed the government's decision to delay the final lifting of lockdown restrictions scheduled for 21 June. Forty-nine Conservative MPs voted against the amendment, including Sir Graham Brady, chair of the 1922 committee, and Mark Harper, chair of the

Covid Recovery Group and former chief whip. While the legislation passed, the size of the rebellion was a warning to the government about the mood of backbenchers towards any similar moves in the future.

- In September 2021, the *London Economic* reported that 10 Conservative MPs had rebelled against the government's Health and Social Care Levy Bill which was brought in to raise £12 billion to fund social care but which broke the Conservatives' 2019 election manifesto commitment not to raise taxes. Rebels included former ministers Esther McVey and Sir Christopher Chope, while many more abstained.

In September 2021 allegations were levelled at Conservative whips from Tory backbenchers that there had been threats to withhold funds for their constituencies if they rebelled on key votes. The revelations led many to condemn the practice.

Box 8.3 Whips and backbenchers

Caroline Slocock, director of the Civil Exchange think tank, commented on allegations related to Conservative whips' tactics in *The Guardian*:

> Every government uses tough tactics to curtail rebellions from its own side on key votes. But it is shocking if government whips are promising to hand out public money (or deny it) to their MPs to buy votes. Public funds should be allocated following clear criteria based on need, with due process. If these allegations are true, the government risks undermining confidence in government — something more important than winning one vote.

Source: 'Tory whips accused of threatening rebels with loss of local funding', *The Guardian*, 15 September 2021

Comparisons and connections

Comparing legislatures in the UK and USA, especially connected to the way that they check and balance the executive branch and in the constitutional arrangements that support them, is a common focus of comparative questions. Traditional similarities and differences have been shown in a new light by notable contemporary events.

The significance of the threat of 'backbench rebellion' in the UK is entirely different to that of the United States of America. While slender or non-existent majorities in the Commons can destabilise and ultimately unseat a British prime minister (who always requires 'the confidence of the House of Commons'), a US president has their own mandate, with a constitutionally separate power base to that of Congress.

However, while the impeachment process can eject US presidents, usually on grounds of corruption or illegal behaviour, partisanship — similar to that of the Commons — plays a crucial part. As a two-thirds Senate majority is required to conclude an impeachment process, several recent attempts have been thwarted. Most notably in 2021, Donald Trump avoided impeachment for 'high crimes and misdemeanours' by two Senate votes after the House had voted to impeach. The 57:43 Senate vote on 13 February 2021 was two votes short of the 59 super-majority needed to successfully impeach.

In addition, the activity of committees plays a part in the strengths and weaknesses of the respective legislatures. There is little doubt that parliament has felt the benefits of a reinvigorated and independent range of departmental select committees unafraid to skewer ministers — such as the then foreign secretary Dominic Raab, who was exposed over the government's handling of the evacuation of Afghanistan in September 2021. Sometimes this has a lasting effect — Raab was replaced by Liz Truss soon afterwards — meaning that the power of select committees is often contrasted with the party-dominated parliamentary Public Bill Committees that can fail to give legislation the objective scrutiny that it needs.

In the USA, the growing partisanship of Congress has appeared to negate many of the previously formidable congressional committees. In 2021, it seemed increasingly evident to many commentators that the Democrat-dominated congressional committees that had pursued Donald Trump's executive with such hostility were far less aggressive to the Biden executive's failings. The *New Yorker* reported in September 2021 that despite the 'deadly surge of COVID-19 in the US and the chaotic American withdrawal from Afghanistan' Congress was largely passive.

What next?

Read: Sir Anthony Seldon's article 'The prime minister and cabinet: theories and myths of executive power' in *Politics Review*, Volume 31, November 2021

Read: Lord Norton of Louth's article 'Parliament and government in the UK: a relationship in flux' in *Politics Review*, Volume 31, April 2021

Research: select committees on the Institute for Government's Parliamentary Monitor 2021

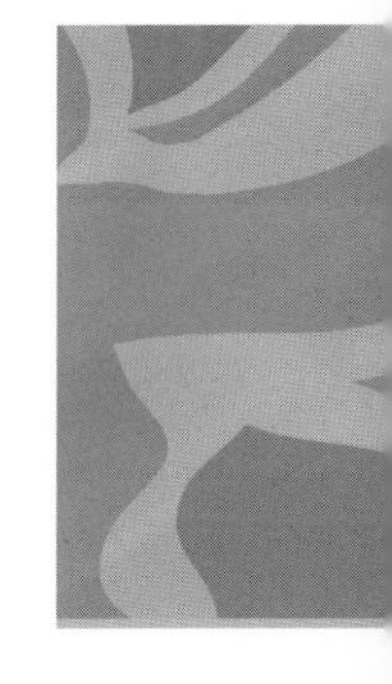

Chapter 9

The House of Lords: the role and impact of peers in the 2020s

Focus

Examination specifications focus on the selection, composition and functions of both Houses of Parliament. For the House of Lords — as for the House of Commons — students require knowledge of how peers are selected and how effective the second chamber is in fulfilling its role — especially in amending and improving legislation.

Edexcel	UK Government 2.1–2.4	Including: structure, role, selection and effectiveness of the House of Lords
AQA	3.1.1.2	Including: role, influence and significance of the House of Lords

Context

The House of Lords remains a controversial and highly contested part of politics in the UK. It is one of very few unelected legislative chambers in the world and consequently, as the UK is a democracy, it is substantially less powerful than its fully elected counterpart, the House of Commons. The main roles of the Lords are to revise and improve legislation and to use its significant expertise through inquiries and reviews into government activity.

The year 2021 saw the unelected nature of the Lords continue to be the subject of sustained scrutiny. If 2020 was the year for controversial prime ministerial appointments to the Lords, in the form of close associates and supporters, in 2021 a larger than ever number of by-elections took place to fill vacancies in the ranks of the 92 hereditary peers. It led *The Times* to demand an answer as to whether it is time to end the 'farce of hereditary peers' who perpetuate 'a system that gives the elite an automatic role in running the country'.

For students of politics, two key current areas of focus are:

1. **The composition and selection of Lords** and the extent to which this further undermines the legitimacy of the second chamber. While the vast majority of peers are ennobled as life peers, the fact that 92 hereditary peers, elected by their 'fellow' Lords after inheriting their titles, can affect legislation is the source of much dispute.
2. **The double-edged debate over the Lords' involvement in the legislative process**. Needless to say, having unelected, unaccountable and unrepresentative legislators actively involved in the process of shaping laws appears to be indefensible. Yet even critics of the Lords accept that many government bills are substantially improved by their involvement. And many peers possess political and constitutional expertise, or have knowledge and experience in fast-changing or relevant areas such as science, business, technology, justice or healthcare — to a level often lacking in the Commons.

Box 9.1 Key definitions

Hereditary peer: a member of the House of Lords with an inherited title. There were more than 800 hereditary peers in the Lords prior to the House of Lords Act 1999. The 1999 Act reduced this to just 92.

Life peer: member of the House of Lords appointed to the second chamber during their lifetime and whose title cannot be inherited.

Selecting the Lords: the election of hereditary peers

Members of the UK's second chamber are not selected in the same way that constituency-elected representatives win their seats in the House of Commons. The vast majority (around 750) of the current members of the House of Lords are life peers, appointed by the queen on the recommendation of successive prime ministers. However, the House of Lords Act 1999 permits 92 hereditary peers to continue to sit in the House of Lords, with by-elections held to fill vacancies when a hereditary peers dies, resigns or is removed for non-attendance.

Box 9.2 Hereditary peer by-elections

By-elections, conducted to replace party/voting allegiance like-for-like (with the electorate drawn from rest of the relevant party's hereditary peers in the House of Lords), must be held within 3 months of a vacancy occurring. Following parliament's suspension on 23 March 2020, successive motions were passed to delay the required by-elections until parliament resumed. The first of these by-elections was held in June 2021.

A total of six vacancies were filled through by-elections in June and July 2021: four Conservative peers; one Labour peer; one cross-bencher. The by-elections were controversial for a number of reasons:

- There was criticism that the 21 candidates who contested the available places to replace the three Conservative hereditary peers were all male, as was the electorate of 43 all-male hereditary Conservative peers (of whom 36 voted).
- Many observers commented on the single candidate who stood unopposed to take the Labour vacancy. The uncontested nature of the election was highlighted, especially as the winner will be able to shape legislation and claim tax-free allowances of up to £323 a day for attending sittings.
- In addition, the identity of the new Labour peer provoked further comment: 'Without even a vote, Tony Benn's son reclaims his family seat in the Lords' reported *The Times* in July 2021. It was widely noted that Stephen Benn had taken up the seat in the House of Lords that his father had renounced. Tony Benn, former Labour MP for Bristol South East for several decades, strongly opposed hereditary peerages, declaring the system 'absolutely mad'.

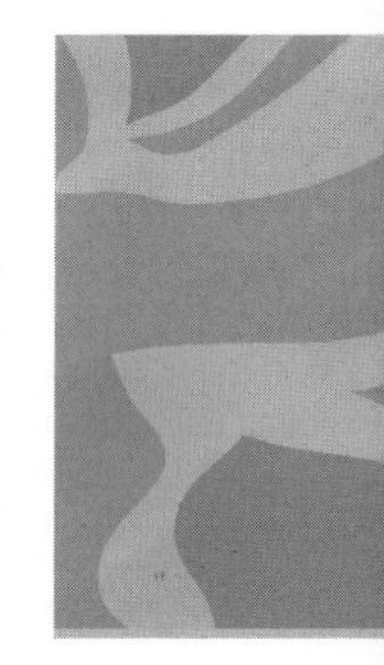

In 2021, the Electoral Reform Society — a long-standing campaign group for democratic reform — used the coronavirus-induced delay to hereditary peer by-elections to campaign for their abolition. When it was finally announced that the hereditary peer by-elections were set to resume, the Electoral Reform Society highlighted the male-dominated list of eligible candidates and the small number of voters permitted to vote, declaring it a further 'testament to the House of Lords being a private members' club for an elite few'.

Box 9.3 The campaign to remove hereditary peer by-elections

Removing these by-elections would be the first step in a package of reform desperately needed to ensure we have a scrutiny chamber that is fit for purpose, rather than this elitist mockery of democracy. These so-called by-elections must be the last. It's time politicians — including the new Lord Speaker — took the steps needed to abolish this absurd practice and give the public a say over who sits in our second chamber.

Willie Sullivan, Senior Director at the Electoral Reform Society, May 2021

While the democratic election (if only on a microscopic scale) to replace hereditary peers draws more attention to the chamber than usual, there remains some support for the relatively small number of hereditary peers who remain in the Lords, with recently ennobled life peer Lord (Charles) Moore writing in *The Spectator* (March 2021) that 'the hereditaries are on average a bit less partisan and more diligent than the average of my own kind'. Lord Moore was referring to the fact that the 92 hereditary peers permitted to continue in the Lords are seen by many as conscientious and attentive legislators.

However, the *Daily Mail* drew further attention to the questionable value of hereditary peers, and *The Scotsman* (July 2021) also highlighted the role that the hereditary peer by-elections play in 'handing aristocrats a significant role in our parliament and over the issues that affect all of our lives...without giving the public any say whatsoever'. Several newspapers ran calculations that compared the 'tax free' daily attendance allowance of £323 for each day that peers usually work in parliament with the 'virtual parliament' allowance of £162, claimed simply 'for tuning in and voting from home'. It was also revealed by the *Mail* that during the 12 months of the health crisis the average hereditary peer voted 113 times out of a possible 143, yet for the same period the previous year, hereditary peers voted just 24 times on average out of a possible 51.

The legislative influence of the House of Lords

The House of Lords plays a significant role in the passage of legislation through the UK Parliament. While the House of Commons remains by far the dominant chamber in Westminster's bicameral (two-chambered) legislature, the Lords can propose amendments to bills passed in the Commons, thereby 'defeating' the government (see Table 9.1), and can delay bills for up to a year — a prospect that can force concessions from the government in order to speed up the legislative process.

The Lords is regularly criticised for its unelected composition. However, the early 2020s demonstrated its value in amending and clarifying legislation, especially in favour of vulnerable social groups, and in encouraging the government to reconsider, or to bring forward further improvement and change, such as improving protection of children in difficult domestic break-ups by strengthening standards in child contact centres (see below).

Box 9.4 The legislative effectiveness of the House of Lords

The House carries out well its role in legislative scrutiny, facilitated by its composition (collectively, no one party having a majority, and individually, with members who have notable experience and expertise) and its procedures (all amendments being considered, no programme motions, any peer able to contribute at committee stage, amendments taken at Third Reading).

Lord Norton of Louth, 'Reforming the House of Lords', 18 July 2021, https://nortonview.wordpress.com

Five ways that the Lords can affect legislation include:

1 **Legislation can be introduced in the House of Lords.** In 2021, constitutional expert Lord Norton of Louth introduced the House of Lords (Peerages Nominations) Bill with the aim of putting the appointment of life peers on a statutory footing and establishing a new commission to better advise the prime minister on making recommendations for life peerages.

2 **The government can accept Lords amendments to improve legislation, especially to protect vulnerable groups.** In April 2021, the government accepted an amendment made in the House of Lords to the Financial Services Bill, which sought to ensure that retailers were able to offer free cash back from tills without requiring a purchase. It was recognised that some groups in society are more reliant on cash than others, and many rural areas lack access to free ATMs (or cashpoints).

3 **Lords committees can conduct and publish inquiries into government bills.** In July 2021 the House of Lords Communication and Digital Committee published the outcome of its inquiry into the government's Online Safety Bill (Online Harms). One prominent conclusion was a warning that the bill posed a 'threat to free speech' through its proposed clampdown on 'legal but harmful' content. While some restrictions — especially over hate speech or dangerous conspiracy theories — were deemed to be necessary, the prospect of automated filtering systems regulating 'normal expressions of negative human thoughts' was reckoned to be 'a nightmare'.

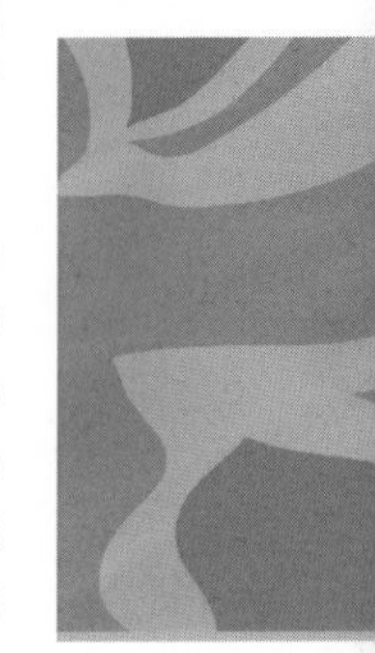

4 **The Lords power of delay can extract compromises from the government.** In April 2021, just days before the parliamentary session was due to end, the Lords finally backed down after their amendments to deal more stringently with stalkers were repeatedly rejected in the House of Commons during the passage of the Domestic Abuse Act 2021. However, in order for the bill to pass, the government made a series of compromises on other proposals by the Lords to better protect children in difficult domestic break-ups by strengthening standards in child contact centres (neutral meeting places for children and parents).

5 **Lords proposals can be rejected, but can bring about future change.** The House of Lords proposed amendments to the Fire Safety Act 2021 to protect leaseholders from the costs of fixing fire-related problems in the wake of the Grenfell Tower disaster. The government rejected the Lords amendments but Home Office minister Kit Malthouse conceded that they were 'well intentioned' and said that the government planned to tackle the question of who should pay in the forthcoming building safety bill.

Table 9.1 Recent notable defeats of the government in the House of Lords

Date	Bill	Reason for defeat
January 2021	Covert Human Intelligence Sources (Criminal Conduct) Bill	The Lords sought to insert a requirement into the bill to ensure that those granting authorisation for operatives involved in covert activity to participate in criminal conduct reasonably believe that the authorisation is necessary and proportionate.
February 2021	Universal Credit Amendment Regulations (2021)	The Lords rejected the bill on the grounds that the regulations do not fully compensate claimants who move from Severe Disability Premium legacy benefits to Universal Credit and called on the government to extend the Covid-19 Universal Credit uplift to legacy benefits.
March 2021	Domestic Abuse Bill	The Lords sought to insert a clause into the bill which required that all victims of domestic abuse, including those with migrant and refugee status, receive equal protection and support.
April 2021	Fire Safety Bill	In light of new fire safety measures introduced in the aftermath of the Grenfell Tower fire, the Lords insisted, for a third time, that building owners should be prevented from passing on costs of work required by the Act to tenants and leaseholders.
July 2021	Coronavirus-related amendments to the Health and Social Care Act	Government legislation to introduce regulations requiring all care workers to be fully vaccinated was rejected by the Lords on the grounds that there was insufficient evidence of the potentially critical impact on staffing levels of permanently requiring health staff to be fully vaccinated.
October 2021	Police, Crime, Sentencing and Courts Bill	Conservative peer Helen Newlove tabled an amendment to the Police, Crime, Sentencing and Courts Bill to challenge the government's stance that misogyny should not be classed as a hate crime.

Comparisons and connections

A common area of contrast between institutions in the UK and USA lies in the bicameral features of their respective legislatures, and between the characteristics and powers of the House of Lords and the Senate in particular. Any similarities are largely overshadowed by the fact that while the houses of the US Congress have broadly equal powers, the UK's House Lords is subordinate to the House of Commons in every way.

Three particular areas of comparison lie in the following:

- **Representation:** the Senate is comprised of 100 members with two elected from each of the 50 US states. Regardless of geographic or population size, all US states have equal representative value in the Senate, meaning that, for example, sparsely populated but agriculturally vital states of the mid-West (such as Kansas, Nebraska and the Dakotas) are as prominently represented as far more populous states. There is no specific 'cap' on the number of Lords and no similar requirement for regional balance. In 2020–21 it is calculated that 55% of peers live in London or the east and southeast of England. Just 6% of peers live in the East and West Midlands.
- **Electoral accountability:** US State senators are directly elected from each state to serve 6-year terms. Roughly a third of senators are up for election every 2 years and in November 2020, there were 35 Senate elections. The majority of peers in the Lords are ennobled for life, formally by the queen but on the advice of the prime minister. From his appointment in 2019, Boris Johnson is averaging 41 appointments per year — a higher average than any of his predecessors since the 1958 Life Peerages Act.
- **Political power:** apart from financial bills, almost all US legislation originates in the Senate, and all legislation must be approved by it. In addition, treaties must be ratified by a two-thirds majority in the Senate, and all of the president's cabinet and judicial appointments (for example US secretary of state Antony Blinken was confirmed by a 78–22 Senate vote in January 2021) need Senate approval by simple majority. On the other hand, the 1911 House of Lords Act was a seminal moment in the history of the Lords, formally reducing its status below the Commons. The Lords still has the power to delay legislation and plays a valuable role in revising and improving government legislation, but cannot block it and plays no role in confirming executive appointments.

Exam success

The role and power of the Lords and the recent attention given to the continuing presence of hereditary peers mean that its 'temporary' status as an unelected chamber and calls for full reform remain areas of significant debate. Questions in this area may be framed as follows:

- *Evaluate the extent to which the House of Lords should become a fully elected second chamber.* (Edexcel-style, 30 marks)
- *'The UK needs a fully elected second chamber.' Analyse and evaluate this statement.* (AQA-style, 25 marks)

The best responses will place recent debates about the selection and composition of the Lords in context with the process of modernisation, evaluating the criteria for liberal democracies and for effective bicameral legislatures. Lords reform commenced in the late 1990s to create a 'transitional' house comprised of life peers and hereditaries, but only until a suitable alternative chamber to the Commons could be agreed on. Since then, the process of reform has stalled. The best essays will therefore focus on the following themes:

- The Lords appointments process is currently unregulated, unconstrained and highly controversial. Accusations of 'cronyism' have been levelled at all prime ministers in their 'logical' appointment of key supporters to the Lords, yet the chamber is often commended for its expertise and legislative value.
- The creation of an elected second chamber is likely to lead to questions over legislative primacy. If a future second chamber is to be regionally representative and elected via a more proportional system, it could claim greater legitimacy than the Commons.
- The expense and inefficiency of bicameral legislatures is contentious. With over 800 current peers alongside 650 commoners, the size of the UK Parliament, especially set against the growing responsibilities of regional assemblies, is substantial. Yet it is difficult to see the executive-dominated UK benefiting from a unicameral legislature.

What next?

Read: Democratic Audit's explanation 'What does democracy require for second chambers in legislatures?', **www.democraticaudit.com** (part of the article 'How undemocratic is the House of Lords?')

Research: Lord Norton's House of Lords (Peerage Nominations) Bill, **https://bills.parliament.uk**, and keep an eye on its parliamentary progress

Chapter 10

The UK Supreme Court: redefining judicial power in the 2020s

Focus

Examination specifications require strong knowledge of the role and composition of the UK Supreme Court and effective analysis of the judiciary's relationship with the executive and parliament. Students also need to understand the doctrine of judicial review, and the extent to which this affects the Supreme Court's interactions with and influence over the legislative and policy-making processes.

Edexcel	UK Government 4.1	The Supreme Court and its interactions with, and influence over, the legislative and policy-making processes
AQA	3.1.1.4	The role of the Supreme Court and its impact on government, legislature and policy process

Context

Declared to be the 'Enemies of the People' in a headline in the *Daily Mail* in 2016, the UK's senior judges have been accused by some of seeking to defy the will of the people — especially in attempting to 'thwart' Brexit and in declaring Boris Johnson's parliamentary prorogation unlawful in 2019.

While the Supreme Court's role in the Brexit process prompted unparalleled media attention, conflict between judges and politicians has been growing for several decades, particularly following the passage of the Human Rights Act in the late 1990s and the creation of the UK Supreme Court itself in 2009.

In response to this, in 2019 the think tank Policy Exchange established its Judicial Power Project to focus on what it considers to be 'judicial overreach' that 'increasingly threatens the rule of law and effective, democratic government'. And in March 2021, the government commissioned an Independent Review of Administrative Law (IRAL) to examine the 'appropriate constitutional place of judicial review'. The judicial branch's role in UK politics has rarely been more contested.

For students of politics, two inter-connected areas of focus are:

- The debate over whether judges have strayed beyond their constitutional remit and into the realms of governing and legislating. The early years of the 2020s have seen a growing resolve on the part of the government to highlight and curb what they consider to be an increasingly powerful, and politicised, judicial branch.
- The contested role of judicial review and the extent to which judges have enhanced their appetite for supervising government activity; whether certain types of executive decisions should be protected from judicial interference and whether the full scope of judicial review should be placed on a clear and statutory footing.

Box 10.1 Key definitions

Politicisation: the process by which individuals or institutions, normally seen as above party-political interests and activities, are drawn into it.

Judicial review: the means by which the courts audit or check the legality of decision-making by public bodies in the UK. It was through the process of judicial review that the Supreme Court judged prime minister Boris Johnson to have unlawfully prorogued (closed down) parliament in 2019.

Box 10.2 Overview: the changing composition of the Supreme Court

Following the retirement of Lady Black in January 2021, Lady Justice Rose joined the UK Supreme Court in April 2021.

The process of appointment to the Supreme Court requires the creation of an independent commission: a five-member group comprising the President of the Supreme Court, the Deputy President of the Supreme Court, one member of the Judicial Appointments Commission (JAC), one member of the Judicial Appointments Board for Scotland, and one member of the Northern Ireland Judicial Appointments Commission.

For potential Supreme Court appointees, Section 25 of the Constitutional Reform Act 2005 sets out the statutory qualifications, including that 'applicants must have held high judicial office for at least two years' or 'have been a qualifying practitioner for at least 15 years'.

The independent commission's recommendation is passed from the prime minister and lord chancellor to the queen, who confirms the appointment. Lady Rose is currently one of just two female Supreme Court justices.

To what extent have judges become too politically powerful?

Judicial power has rarely been more contested than it is in the 2020s. Many people, including figures within the current Conservative government, believe the judicial branch has become too 'expansive', that is to say, that judges go beyond the legal and constitutional remit of an independent judiciary that settles disputes fairly. Instead, they have taken on the responsibility of overseeing parliament's legislative actions and of supervising the executive's exercise of its lawful powers — in the words of *Prospect Magazine*'s Alexander Horne (August 2021), 'failing to respect the legislature's final authority, or the executive's exercise of its powers'.

Factors contributing to claims that judges have become 'too powerful' include:

- **Undermining parliament's legislative supremacy**. As a democratically elected institution, parliament is best placed to legislate in keeping with the rule of law. While governments and ministers are accountable to both parliament and the people, judges are not. Yet in 2017, the number of cases decided by the Supreme Court rose to a record 109, compared to just 75 in 2016 and 83 in 2015. While recent years have seen a fall in cases decided by the Supreme Court (to some extent as a consequence of the health crisis), in the aftermath of the highly contested Brexit vote, it appeared to many that the Supreme Court was seeking to assert itself in the face of an unstable and uncertain parliament that lacked its traditional authority.

- **Policing the executive's use of its constitutional powers**. While there are very few states with uncodified constitutions, where they do exist, responsibility and restraint are key characteristics of government. In the UK, some claim that the scope of judicial activity has widened to the extent that the judiciary has, at times, 'policed' what has traditionally been seen as the executive's constitutional responsibility. For some, the precedent-setting role that the Supreme Court played in overturning Boris Johnson's decision to prorogue parliament in 2019 reveals an inclination for judges to stray into territory that is 'not for the courts'.
- **Following America's 'constitutional court' model**. The US Supreme Court has developed a tradition of judicial activism and self-confidence over several centuries. Critics of UK Supreme Court activity see a rapid acceleration towards a US-style constitutional court. Unlike the USA, the UK has neither a codified constitution nor a clear separation between the branches of government. A succession of relatively weak governments — coalitions, and ones with slender or non-existent majorities — has provided an environment for a judicial branch to assert itself, becoming, in the words of the Institute for Government's Raphael Hogarth (2019), 'a guardian of democracy in the UK, policing the boundaries of constitutionally proper behaviour'.

What is judicial review and why is it so controversial?

Judicial review is the process by which the lawfulness of decisions made by central or local government, or agencies of state such as regulators, is challenged. It is a controversial process because it frequently pits the judicial branch against the government, with senior judges often overturning ministerial decisions, leading to frustration and suspicion. In 2020, the former Supreme Court justice Lord Sumption argued that there was evidence of 'excessive and inappropriate use of judicial review' to overturn government ministers' decisions.

Box 10.3 The scope and growth of judicial review

In contrast to the current crop of senior judges, Lord Lexden also noted that 'the next generation [of judges] coming up are more cautious about operation of their powers'. The data appears to support this view, and Bar Council figures indicate that applications for judicial review fell by 44% between 2015 and the end of September 2019 (figures in 2020 and 2021 were affected by the health pandemic).

In 2013, access to judicial review was substantially restricted by the coalition government when it limited the right to use legal aid for challenges and raised court fees. Nevertheless, between 2014 (the first full year of figures) and 2019, applications for judicial review averaged around 11,300 claims per year. The Institute for Government revealed that in 2020 the Home Office alone faced 842 judicial review applications and the Ministry of Justice faced 750 cases.

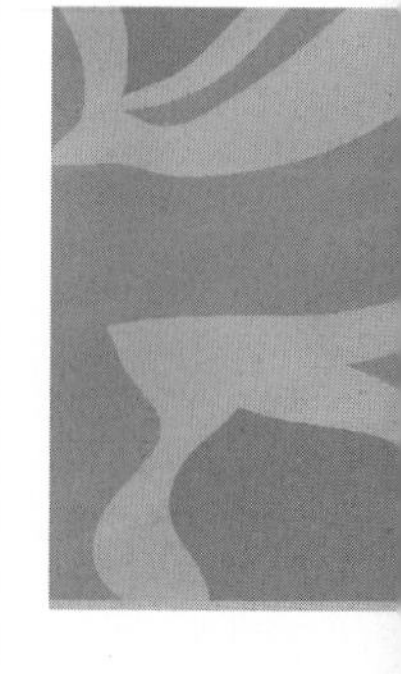

There are three main grounds for challenging a government decision by judicial review. In addition, the threat of judicial review can influence government action too.

1 **Procedural unfairness:** if the process by which a decision is made is considered to be improper. In July 2021 the Department for Work and Pensions (DWP) agreed to change its 'unfair, unlawful and discriminatory' pressuring of benefits claimants to drop tribunals. The DWP frequently engaged in the practice of making last-minute higher benefit offers to claimants (though still lower than a legal entitlement). The department finally agreed to change its practices the day before a judicial review into its activity was due to commence.

2 **Unreasonableness or irrationality:** while it is rare for the courts to grant judicial review on this basis, in July 2021 the education secretary's refusal to revoke an order imposed on a primary school to become an academy was declared 'irrational' by the High Court after the school's governors brought a judicial review of the decision. After considering the 'clear evidence from the school and the local authority of both continued efforts to improve and success in achieving those improvements' the court quashed the academy order, refused an application from the education secretary, Gavin Williamson, for permission to appeal and ordered him to pay the school costs of £75,000.

3 **Illegality:** such as if a decision contravenes existing law. In March 2021 *The Guardian* reported that 'the government will be in clear breach of the law and exposed to a judicial review' through the abandonment of its commitment to spend 0.7% of national income on overseas aid. In the aftermath of the cuts, several charities, including the International Planned Parenthood Federation, notified the government of their intention to seek a judicial review after the Foreign Office told them it was terminating their project funding.

How and why is the government seeking to curb judicial power?

The 2019 Conservative manifesto paved the way for future legislative activity to address the scope of judicial power. The Tory manifesto stated that 'after Brexit we need to look at the relationship between the government, parliament and the courts', and in July 2021, the government introduced the Judicial Review and Courts Bill in parliament.

Amongst other proposals, the Judicial Review and Courts Bill sought, in the government's words, 'to create a better balance between the rights of citizens to challenge executive decisions through judicial review and the need for effective government'. According to the lord chancellor, Robert Buckland, its main objective was to ensure that judges are 'cautious in their decision-making and to ensure that their judgements properly reflect the intent of our elected parliament'. The implied criticism of judges is that they had failed to 'keep pace' with the 'popular' democratic changes that had delivered the Brexit vote and swept Boris Johnson to power.

However, being referred to by some as a 'solution without a problem', critics of the government's legislative proposals see it as an unnecessary and undemocratic move:

- Writing on the website **www.politics.co.uk**, Ian Dunt sees it as part of 'a pattern of government activity' and 'a consistent and perpetual attempt to silence or hamstring the institutions which might restrain its power'.
- A cross-party group of MPs and peers wrote to the lord chancellor in June 2021, saying that legislative moves to restrict judicial review were 'an affront to the principles of fairness and government accountability' and should be dropped (see Box 10.4).

Box 10.4 Opposition to the government's proposals to limit judicial review proposals

In June 2021, the Liberal Democrat leader, Ed Davey, together with Labour's Clive Lewis, the SNP's Joanna Cherry QC, the Green MP Caroline Lucas and 28 others wrote to the lord chancellor about the planned reforms, asserting that:

> The proposals would weaken both individuals and the courts, and effectively put government actions beyond the reach of the law. Together, these changes would make it much harder for people to put things right when mistakes are made or governments overstep their bounds. They would undermine the rule of law and the crucial principles of fairness and accountability.

- In April 2021, the Law Society's president I. Stephanie Boyce criticised the way that the government's legislation had deviated substantially from the advice it received from the expert panel in its planning stages (Box 10.5).

Box 10.5 Government 'over-reach'?

> The Ministry of Justice has gone beyond what was recommended by the expert panel set up to advise it, with no evidence to back up this over-reach. The effect of the proposals would be a fundamental distortion of the protection judicial review is supposed to provide against state action, undermining the rule of law and restricting access to justice.

The Law Society president I. Stephanie Boyce

Comparative exam success

The judiciary offers an attractive topic for drawing comparisons between political activity and institutional power in the UK and USA. Comparative examination questions may be framed as follows:

- *Examine how the Supreme Court in the USA is more powerful than its UK counterpart.* (Edexcel short response, 12 marks)
- *'The US Supreme Court is significantly more powerful than its UK equivalent.' Analyse and evaluate this statement.* (AQA long response, 9 marks)

The constitutional context of the USA and UK provides the key to evaluating the relative powers of their supreme courts. As 'guardians' of the (codified) constitution, US Supreme Court justices can effectively determine the limits of presidential, congressional and state powers through their power of judicial review — the capacity to make judgements that can only be overturned by later Court rulings or by constitutional amendments.

- **Example:** in September 2021 the Supreme Court ruled by a narrow 5–4 majority that a Texas law banning all abortions after 6 weeks of pregnancy could go into effect.

On the contrary, in the UK the Supreme Court is no match for a government with a healthy Commons majority. While the UK Supreme Court can declare actions illegal — and in general governments will wish to follow those rulings — there are examples of governments ignoring Supreme Court rulings, or passing retrospective legislation to legalise previously illegal activity.

- **Example:** when the government lacks parliamentary support, it is forced to comply with rulings against it, such as when the Supreme Court ruled in 2019 that parliament's prorogation was illegal. However, the advent of the Judicial Review and Courts Bill in 2021 reflects the ability of the UK government to redefine judicial power.

In addition to the above:

- **Rational approaches** to comparing US and UK courts will develop the political and philosophical stances of the judges in their administration of justice.
- **Cultural approaches** focus on the significant differences in the history, legitimacy and acceptance of court activity. While the US Supreme Court has reviewed the activity of other government branches for over two centuries, the UK's Supreme Court's is less than two decades old.
- **Structural approaches** highlight substantial differences in the processes of judicial appointment and in court compositions as well as the constitutional differences in the two states.

What next?

Read: the Institute for Government's 'Judicial review and policy making: the role of legal advice in government', April 2021, **www.instituteforgovernment.org.uk**

Follow: the progress of the Judicial Review and Courts Bill, **https://bills.parliament.uk/bills/3035**